TESSERAE

BOOKS BY DENISE LEVERTOV

POETRY

The Double Image
Here and Now
Overland to the Islands
With Eyes at the Back of Our Heads
The Jacob's Ladder
O Taste and See
The Sorrow Dance
Relearning the Alphabet
To Stay Alive
Footprints
The Freeing of the Dust
Life in the Forest
Collected Earlier Poems 1940-1960
Candles in Babylon
Poems 1960-1967
Oblique Prayers
Poems 1968-1972
Breathing the Water
A Door in the Hive
Evening Train

PROSE

Poet in the World
Light Up the Cave
New & Selected Essays
Tesserae

TRANSLATIONS

Guillevic/Selected Poems
Joubert/Black Iris (Copper Canyon Press)

DENISE LEVERTOV

TESSERAE

MEMORIES & SUPPOSITIONS

A NEW DIRECTIONS BOOK

Grateful acknowledgment is made to the editors and publishers of *The American Poetry Review* and *New Directions in Prose and Poetry* which first published some of the pieces in this collection.

Book design by Sylvia Frezzolini Severance
Manufactured in the United States of America
New Directions Books are printed on acid-free paper
First published clothbound in 1995
First published as New Directions paperbook 832 in 1996.

Published simultaneously in Canada by Penguin Books Canada Limited

Library of Congress Cataloging-in-Publication Data

Levertov, Denise, 1923–
    Tesserae : memories & suppositions / Denise Levertov.
        p.   cm.
    ISBN 0–8112–1337–4 (pbk.)
    1. Levertov, Denise, 1923–   —Biography.   2. Women poets,
American—20th century—Biography.   I. Title.
[PS3562.E8876Z47   1996]
811'.54—dc20   96–23850
[B]   CIP

Celebrating sixty years of publishing for James Laughlin
by New Directions Publishing Corporation,
80 Eighth Avenue, New York, NY 10011

◆ AUTHOR'S NOTE

These tesserae have no pretensions
to forming an entire mosaic.
They are merely fragments,
composed from time to time
in between poems.

CONTENTS

TESSERAE

THE SACK FULL OF WINGS

When my father was a little boy in Russia an old pedlar used to come by from time to time, carrying a big sack over his shoulder. Sometimes he would be seen in the streets and outlying districts of the town of Orsha, my father's home; sometimes when my father was taken to the larger city of Vitepsk to visit his grandparents and uncles, there again he would glimpse the pedlar, trudging along, always carrying his bulky sack. My father did not wonder what was in the sack, for he believed he knew: it was full of wings, wings which would enable people to fly like birds. (Of my father's great-grandfather, the Rav of Northern White Russia, it was told that although when young he had abjured the temptation to learn the language of birds, yet in old age he understood all that they said.)

When my father was ten years old another boy was born in Vitepsk who grew up to become a great and renowned painter: Marc Chagall. He and my father never knew one another, but Chagall depicted the old pedlar and his sack. He is flying, though not with wings. Perhaps the constant burden of such a concentration of wings was transmuted into the ability to levitate without stretching and flapping a single pair of them. At all events, it is clearly the same man, exactly as my father used to describe him when I was a child in London and he a middle-aged Anglican parson. I didn't discover until after my father's death in 1954 that Chagall had shared his recognition of the sack's magic.

INHERITANCE

In 1890, when my mother was five years old, staying with her grandmother in Caernarvon, North Wales, she was taken on a day's visit to an ancient great-uncle who lived alone by the sea, somewhere along the Caernarvonshire coast. His tiny whitewashed cottage had only one room, but that room was clean and neat and a kettle steamed on the hob. The floor was of earth, compacted, and decorated each day with patterns made by squeezing green juice from certain leaves. He had a long white beard, and wore knee-britches. His legs and feet were bare, for he had been mending his fishing nets on the strand. My mother's grandmother told her to remember what he said, and she did, although it was a number of years before she understood its interest: he recounted how he had been at the Battle of Waterloo, and had seen Napoleon—Boney himself—ride away on his towering horse. So I, living in the age of jets and nukes, am separated only by the life span of one person, my mother, from looking into the eyes of a relative who had seen the Emperor at the moment of his defeat; and whose mode of life differed in few respects from that of some ancestor of his (and mine) long before the Norman conquest.

A MINOR ROLE

One day when he was eight or nine my father was walking home from the river, where he had been playing a forbidden game with some other boys. It was the time of year when winter and spring struggle with one another. On the shady side of every house there were great mounds of frozen snow, but in other places there were puddles where the snow had melted. The ice on the wide, swift Dnieper River was breaking up, and the boys had been leaping from floe to floe, riding the ice down-stream for short distances, then jumping back against the current. If a floe split beneath a rider's feet, or if he missed his footing and fell between two of the heavy, moving masses into the black reawakened water, woe betide him.

As he trudged homeward my father's eye was caught by a scrap of printed paper lying in the gray, trampled snow. Though he was a playful, disobedient boy like any other, he was also—like his playmates—a little Talmud scholar, respectful of words; and he saw at a glance, too, that this paper was not printed in Russian but in Hebrew. So he picked it up and began to read. Could it be a fragment of Torah? Never before had he read such a story: about a boy like himself who—it said—was found in the Temple expounding the scriptures to the old, reverent, important rabbis!

My father took the scrap—it was obviously a page from a book—home to his father. The effect was startling. No one asked him where he had been, so his disobedience—risking his life once more in the strictly prohibited game of ice-floe riding—went unnoticed. (He would not have lied.) Instead, his father became angry—not with him, exactly, but rather with the text he had brought to show him. He tore it into pieces and thrust them into the stove. My father was vehemently told to avoid such writings, utterly, if ever he should again encounter them; but just what they were, and how to tell them from holy writ, was not explained. My father was awed to see written words destroyed— Hebrew words. It was not as if it had been a mere scrap of Russian newspaper.

Secretly, he wished he had not given up the mysterious fragment. Who was the wise boy in the story? Yet he knew he ought not to wonder. It was wrong; but he could not forget it. It was wrong the way his desire for a certain very beautiful holy book, a tractate, displayed in the bookseller's window, had been—for that desire had been so powerful it led him to steal a silver ruble from his father in order to buy it. The bookseller had taken the money, but then, looking at him over his spectacles, announced that he would not give him the book before consulting his father. He'd known the money was not his own! That was the only time, then or later, my father ever stole anything; it was the great episode of shame in all his childhood; and he had been forgiven, at last, only because the object of his dishonesty was so understandably tempting, a text of great virtue upon such fine paper, the whole book piously produced.

In the years of seminary study at Volójine, a brilliant and devoted young scholar, my father realized that the scrap of paper must have been part of one of those tales of false Messiahs of which he had heard by then. Even so, he could not help, now and again, wondering wistfully what the rest of the story might have been. It was not until his father sent him (a precocious graduate of the Jewish seminary) out of the country to obtain, as well, a university education (unavailable then to Jews in Russia), that he discovered the identity of the learned child in the Temple. At Königsberg, suddenly free of Tzarist restrictions, he encountered a world of cafés and open lectures and libraries and concerts, a world where Jews and Gentiles mingled in bewildering freedom.

True, his father had read Russian writers—Gogol, Turgeniev, Pushkin—and discussed them with one or two Gentile friends. He had driven out with his father to the nearby estates of these men—liberal aristocrats, members of the intelligentsia, who served on the Zemstvo and tried to give a better life to the peasants; Gentiles who deplored the pogroms. But all of that was exceptional. Such people were rare; his father's friendship with them was almost unprecedented; and that a learned Jew, unworldly though well-to-do, and related to a great Hassidic master, should read secular Russian literature was rarest of all. But here in Prussia, at a great university, much that was strange to my father was taken for granted, and much seemed possible and not sinful that would have horrified him before.

So it was that—not without trepidation, yet with some sense of urgency and inevitability—realizing that what he had stumbled upon as a child must have been the book Gentiles called "the Gospels," he decided to see exactly what this mysterious forbidden text contained. He was, after all, already acquainted with the Cabala; unsophisticated in worldly matters though he was (and in most respects remained all his life), he was both intellectually precocious and secure in his beliefs, so that he felt himself beyond the need for prohibition. And in the Gentile, utterly secular atmosphere of the Prussian city, this book of the Christians seemed more his than theirs. He read it in German, then in Hebrew (for the missionary societies left Hebrew editions of it lying, as it were, in wait for curious young Jews). And as he read he experienced a profound and shaking new conviction. This Jesus of Nazareth "despised and rejected of men," had indeed been the Messiah! A grievous, grievous error had been made. Possessed by his new, extraordinary conviction, shining with faith, he rushed back home—the long train journey south—to share his marvellous discovery with his family, and especially with his father, who though a pious scholar had, after all, desired for this son of his broad knowledge and a questing mind.

Alas, his family was appalled. When my father met his father's fury staunchly, it was decided in despair that he must be mad, and he was locked into his bedroom.

He climbed through the window in the middle of the night and caught the train to Petersburg, and so back to Königsberg.

Soon it became known in Evangelical circles there that a young Russian Jew of good education and prosperous background was being prepared for baptism. This event took place, and my father was, in a small way, lionized. Funds from home ceased to arrive, but he was a brilliant student and easily supported himself at this time by tutoring and undertaking translations to and from the various languages he knew, which already included Russian, German, Hebrew, Aramaic, and Greek. (He later learned English, Latin, and Arabic.) The society into which, on becoming a Christian, he had entered was unfortunately a narrow one, *echt Deutsch* and of a strait-laced piety; and it was eager not to lose its somewhat exotic prize, so different in style and appearance from the Jews of the Polish urban ghettoes and the *schtetels,* with whom these bourgeois Königsbergers would not have mixed socially even if one of them had been a baptized and confirmed Christian.

It was arranged for my father to lodge in the house of one of the Evangelical pastors who had assisted at his baptism; and such was the growing academic success of the young man as time passed, and so evidently sincere his piety (for indeed, he simply continued in the disciplined fervor of his own cultural and familial tradition), that despite his Jewish birth this pastor began to think of him as a highly eligible son-in-law.

The pastor's older daughter was delighted. She had

indeed, already, an eye for my father, who, though not tall, was handsome, with curly dark hair, deep-set dark eyes, and rosy cheeks. It is possible that she was not sorry his nose had a quite non-semitic shape. Her good Papá and Mamá took every opportunity to leave the young folk together—chaperoned, of course, by the younger daughter, who had her own ideas on the subject. The pastor managed to convince himself that my father was in love with his first-born; and she was happy to be convinced likewise. She began to embroider a pair of slippers for him. When the slippers had been presented—as a Christmas gift, received therefore without undue surprise—and the months passed, and still my father did not ask for the hand of the pastor's daughter, the good man decided he no doubt felt unworthy. He tried to encourage him by depicting in glowing terms the security and comfort of a German academic career to which he was sure my father could in time attain. Or he might be blessed to take holy orders, which would be even better. "Then indeed you would be like a son to me," exclaimed this Prussian "Mr. Collins." But my father, though he looked thoughtful and pleased to hear voiced that possibility of ordination which was already his private dream, still did not take the hint. So the pastor, taking the bull by the horns, imparted to him the information that he would not spurn his proposal, and that his timidity, though due to a commendable modesty, was without cause. "In fact, my dear boy, I can whisper it to you that my little pigeon, my Trudi, is ready to receive you kindly," he declared, wiping a tear from his pale blue eye, and taking my father's expression for amazed delight.

My father was not only astonished, he was horrified. Had his father not sent him to the University, but only to the seminary, he would no doubt have been married by this time, to a maiden of good Hassidic antecedents who would have made a home for him while he pursued the study of Torah and Talmud and Zohar for the rest of his life. His Destiny had already made that impossible; but though his energies had been channelled into an even more intense devotion to study—he was reading philosophy, history, church history, Christian theology, applying to them all the concentration of a young rabbi—he had his own vague dream of a wife, and she was not a Fraulein Gertrud with her pale stare and harsh Prussian voice.

It was not easy to make the Pastor understand that my father did not wish for the privilege of becoming his son-in-law, but when he finally grasped the fact his jovial sentimentality changed to fury. He expressed sentiments unbecoming to a man of God, and he expressed them loudly. They had been talking in the dining room, with its massive cupboards and a big table, covered between meals with a carpet, around which the young ladies and their mother used to sit with their needlework in the mornings. My father, leaving the pastor thumping on this table till the lamp in the middle of it rattled all the beads of its elaborate shade, rushed upstairs to his bedroom and began stuffing books and clothing haphazard into his trunk.

Where should he go? He must leave this narrow,

cloying, and essentially hypocritical society. His religious faith was intense and unwavering—but it was not in order to be absorbed into a Gentile world that he had broken, in sorrow, with his father and mother, but to be, as he believed, the more fully a Jew. In taking, at baptism, the name of Paul, he had expressed his sense of affinity with the most passionately Jewish of Apostles; he was—and was to so refer to himself all his life—a *Jewish Christian*. Where should he go? He would go to Jerusalem: an old longing, and now was the time to fulfill it.

He did indeed go there, and taught little boys in a church school; and after a time, as an itinerant lecturer, a kind of nineteenth-century Wandering Scholar, travelled from there to Constantinople, where he met my mother—Miss Beatrice Spooner-Jones from Holywell, North Wales. Thus Celt and Jew met in Byzantium.

And it occurs to me, thinking back on their converging paths, to wonder what became of Fraulein Gertrud, but for whom, after all, the chord of Paul and Bee's meeting might never have been struck.

A DUMBSHOW

In 1909 my mother set out from Holywell, North Wales, for Constantinople. She had wanted to go to Paris but her uncle, a Congregational minister who was her guardian, believed Paris was too dangerous a place for a young lady. He consented to her departure for Constantinople because she was to teach at the Scotch Mission School there. Hitherto she had not been outside of Wales except to Chester and Liverpool, and briefly to Edinburgh to be interviewed for this position. The day before her departure from Holywell to so exotic a destination as Constantinople, the old washerwoman (who used to say proudly of her exceedingly sturdy daughter, "Porridge made them legs") exclaimed to my mother, "Oh Miss Jones, I do admire your *bravety*!"

Every aspect of the journey, first to London and then through the Austro-Hungarian Empire, was intensely interesting to the young Welsh lady. When she reached Budapest on the Orient Express, she was met by representatives of the Scottish Church and escorted to their home-in-exile to spend the night. Early next day, her mind and senses full of the adventures of travel, of people and scenes, sounds and smells, all new to her, she woke very early. It was the first time she had ever spent a night on so high a storey as the missionary's flat. All was quiet, and, afraid to wake her hosts but eager to see as much of her surroundings as she could, she raised the unfamiliar Venetian blinds (previously encountered only in novels), and looked forth into the summer morning from her lofty window. Below was an empty street much wider than any she had ever seen before: a boulevard, no doubt. Small trees were planted at intervals along its sidewalks. The buildings opposite were, like the one she was in, massive blocks of flats with ornate entrances. The façade of the one directly across the broad street was punctuated by little balconies; and after a while she was amused to see a maid servant come out onto one of these with a feather bed, which she hung on the balustrade to air in the sunshine. In the British Isles it was "simply *not done*" to thus display bed-linen—above all at the front windows: it suggested fleas! But here the maid brought out another feather bed; and next she returned with a huge pillow, and rested that too on the balcony's wide balustrade. Then there was a pause; she had disappeared through the French doors again, presumably to fetch the second pillow. My mother remained at her window, glad of this brief stillness after days of travel and noise, with more soon to follow. She enjoyed the spaciousness, the elegance, the strangeness. A few plumes of smoke rose into the wide unclouded sky; shadows were still long, the sun already brilliant on the balconied façade. But now came someone along the street: a little girl, nine or ten years old, bustling along, wearing a shawl and an apron—a working-class child, all alone. And just as my mother was dreamily thinking, "A Hungarian child—I'm in Budapest, looking at a Hungarian child—I'm hundreds and hundreds of miles from home"; just as the little girl was about to pass under the airing bedclothes: what should happen but that the balanced pillow, as if by its own volition, all at once slipped off the balustrade and fell—plump!—right in front of her. The child stopped dead—my mother seemed to see her gasp, though all was seen in dumbshow, clear-cut in silence. Then in a flash she looked up: no one; looked round: no one; swooped upon the pillow, almost as big as herself, and clutching the prize with both arms, darted along the street and turned the corner. At the very instant my mother glimpsed her vanishing heels, out came the maid onto the balcony with another pillow—saw the first had gone—leaned over to see the sidewalk—no pillow—rushed back indoors—rushed out again—gestured wild dismay—all the while quite unaware anyone was watching. The distance between my mother and the maid was too great for her to have called across in explanation, even if they had had a common language; besides, though she could not exactly approve, her sympathies were with the little girl. It was a fine, fat pillow; no doubt filled with softest goosedown.

If that child is still alive, over eighty years old at this moment when I write, I daresay she remembers the little drama, and whatever events in her life it may have led to. Did she get a beating or a reward? Was it sold, or kept for someone in her family to sleep on? All her life, and all my mother's life, its sudden appearance at her feet was a picture vivid to their inner eyes, though each witnessed it from a different angle. To the maid and to her mistress—summoned to the balcony in her dressing-gown to gaze up and down the empty street—the pillow might have seemed magicked away, as if its case had dissolved and its feathers had floated like thistledown up and away over the rooftops.

CORDOVA

The smell of ironing—just on the edge of scorch. Where the iron is tried out it leaves its brown silhouette on the ironing-sheet if it's too hot. A sizzle as a drop of water or spit, to see if it's hot *enough,* is applied. These are the old flat-irons, heated on the coal range which was taken out when I was six or seven. But they could still be heated on the new gas stove. Each had a trivet to hold it as an ironed garment or other item was turned over and then put aside, completed. Under the sheet, on the white scrubbed pine kitchen table (never an ironing board), an old cotton blanket folded in several thicknesses provides an "underlay." It is green—two faded shades of green with some beigy cream woven into its pattern. And I see that same pattern if I squeeze my eyes very tight shut, to capture the bright sunlight that comes through closed lids. The color's different, but the pattern's the same.

My mother lets me help by giving me a stack of freshly-ironed handkerchiefs to take upstairs to the bedroom chests of drawers where they belong—Daddy's, hers, Olga's, mine. I am a messenger with important secret papers to deliver. It is a long, dangerous journey. Down the long road—the corridor—with its treacherous corner, into the open space that is the front hall, then the climb which could be a mountain or the stairs of a castle—perhaps with a pause to reconnoitre through the bits of coloured glass in the landing window which give glimpses of a ruby world or a sapphire one, or, through a thick circle of plain glass, a world in which everything is reduced to fairy size.

Once upstairs, I was in a place which was related somehow to the pattern woven into the ironing blanket and into my tight-shut eyes; a city of narrow streets, high walls flush with the street, broken by sudden dark alleys, mysterious doorways, steep ascending stairs. And these streets, except here and there where a bit of sky could be seen, had *roofs*—so it was a place simultaneously indoors and outdoors. There were crowds of shadowy people thronging these lanes; I had to slink along surreptitiously, bearing my precious messages which must not fall into the wrong hands yet must not be crumpled. Sudden brilliant light from those bits of hot blue sky made one squint, and then the deep shade of the roofed street resumed and it was harder to see than before. It seemed there were ways in which one could dodge, by stairways and hidden courtyards, from one building to another and even—because of the roofs—from a building on one side of the street to one on the other. Sometimes there were rugs underfoot instead of paving-stones, or rugs hanging in front of cave-like doors. It was a Casbah!—but I had never heard of a Casbah nor, to my knowledge, had I seen any picture of such a place. The Arabian Nights spoke of a marketplace in which it was easy to get lost, but described no details of its appearance.

At what age did I take in the fact that my father's family came from Cordova (which they left when the Jews were expelled from Spain at the end of the fifteenth century)? I may have heard it in infancy, but it could not have evoked any picture until long afterward. I imagined this place before I attached the name of Cordova to it, but at some point in my childhood I did so. Any concept of the Moorish architecture of Southern Spain in the centuries when Jews, Moors, and Christians coexisted peaceably, and attained such heights of art and scholarship, was decades ahead. Yet the blanket's pattern (and the private pattern inside my closed eyelids) was not only an intimate part of my "handkerchief game" but is re-evoked by Moorish tiles in museums and photographs. In my teens I saw *Pepé le Moko* (and later, *Casablanca*) and recognized that this street had formed part of a Casbah. I've never been to Cordova and don't know if it has a Casbah, but I'm sure it had one in the 1400's.

A photo taken by Peter Brown in the 1980's shows a pattern of coloured light on textured surfaces: gazing at it, I smelled scorched cloth, heard the sizzle of a drop of spit and the clank of iron on trivet. Albeniz evokes the courtyard that may lie beyond one of those great doors flush with the street of teeming shadows; a film of John Williams playing this music in Seville adds another layer to the atmosphere of my game, my renewable *déjà vu.*

Often the exiled Jewish families of Spain took with them the keys to their houses, generation after generation hoping to return. Sometimes a key's purpose would fade from memory, but it would nevertheless be cherished, an ancestral relic, as Marranos cherished shreds of Sabbath ritual centuries after their Jewish origin had been erased from consciousness. I believe that in me an atavistic shred of kinesthetic impressions has persistent life, activated by an old cotton blanket frayed at the edges, and a little task which a child's imagination transformed into an adventure.

AT TAWSTOCK

The real castle, with the battlemented tower and little slits for shooting arrows from, was a ruin. But the huge house was called a castle anyway. We were there because Sir Basil, a Member of Parliament, was a devout churchman and lent his place each year to a clergy family for their summer holidays. Much of the house was closed—windows shuttered, furniture covered in dustcloths. But a drawing room and dining room and a sunny morning-room were open for us, and upstairs, off a long corridor, a whole choice of bedrooms—though my sister and I shared one, as it was thought I might be scared on my own. We occupied an enormous four-poster bed, with a bolster down the middle to keep us from kicking each other.

It was in the castle's woods, as we took one of our family walks, that I heard the dreadful scream, a searing, terrifying sound. My father and sister and I were aghast as much at its unknown origin as at the horror of the sound itself; but my mother knew country things and was able to account for it: the cry of a rabbit caught by a weasel or stoat. It was here at the Home Farm that I was shown a new litter of Black Berkshire piglets and told I could take one home to London when we left. When our departure day rolled round three weeks later, I asked for my pig, only to find the farmer had spoken in jest. I cried all the way back from Devonshire, deprived of my PigWig, the very image of Pigling Bland's sweetheart in my favorite of all Beatrix Potter's stories.

There must have been a huge staff of servants when the family was in residence. There were whole wings of the house we never saw. In the corridor onto which our bedrooms opened, there were little card-holders on the doors, some of them empty but others still holding their cards with the names of guests from the most recent house party—Lady This and Lord That. Most of the doors opened to bedrooms, but some to lavatories or bathrooms; the lavatory (or in American English, toilet) designated to our use had the name of Lord Melchett on its door, and for a couple of years after that we would say at home before we went out, "Just a minute, I have to see Lord Melchett first," instead of the usual euphemism, "I must visit my aunt."

Usually, for our summer holidays, my father would take a *locum tenens* in some country parish, conducting Sunday services and the occasional funeral while the rector and his family went off to London, or the seaside, or perhaps Brittany or Madeira if he had a good stipend. This arrangement gave us a whole house to ourselves, usually a big one, though it wasn't a complete holiday for my mother who still had the shopping and meals and basic housekeeping to think of. But at the castle she was completely free, for once. Though most of the servants were also given their holidays at this time (or some, perhaps, were transferred to Sir Basil's townhouse), a cook and a couple of maids and a butler were left to look after us, and all Mother had to do was discuss the day's menu with the cook. The grounds were enormous, the weather fine, and we took a picnic lunch with us most days—for fun, and to give as little trouble to the staff as possible.

If we didn't feel like a long ramble, there were beautiful formal gardens, lawns, tall clipped hedges, sundials . . . . Of all those dreamy days, one remains the most palpable to me: my father and Olga had gone off on a long walk and my mother and I were sitting in the gardens very peacefully. A great velvety expanse of rolled green lawn stretched away and away from us towards a lush tall thicket of dark shrubs. It was a day deliciously hot in the sun, refreshing in the shade; in the background the constant "midsummer hum," with the occasional mild crescendo of a passing bumblebee. Near us, a flight of stone steps led up to a terrace and to the house itself. My mother, in a shady hat, was sitting in a low comfortable deck chair, and I (still too young to wander off on exploratory expeditions) was playing on the ground at her feet. She was reading, or perhaps was just about to read aloud to me. But she needed a handkerchief and had come out without one. "Just run up and get me a hankie, Den, there's a good child," she said to me. "There are some in the top drawer of the dressing table in my room, right on top, you'll find them easily." So I got up and climbed the broad, shallow steps—the stone was sun-warmed when I put my hand on the balustrade—and crossed the paved terrace and went in by the open double doors and through a space that was dark because outdoors the sunlight was so bright, to the wide hallway from which the stairs mounted to the bedroom corridor. It was cold and silent inside the big house. I went up the wide, carpeted stairs and down the long corridor with its many doors to left and right. Here was my mother's room on the right: I turned the doorknob, opened the door and— ! Oh! Oh! *Not* her bedroom, not a bedroom at all, no four-poster or anything, but *OWLS!* The room was full of owls, owls and other big nameless birds, all motionless, all staring and glaring at me, baleful, indignant! I stood gasping, the doorknob still in my hand, as motionless for an instant as if I myself were stuffed; then slammed the door and fled—along the corridor, lickety-split down the staircase, across the hall and the nameless space and into the never, ever before, so bright and glorious sunlight. I crossed the terrace still at high speed, and ran down the stone steps to the strip of crunchy gravel and the green grass at my mother's feet, and flung myself down, heart pounding.

"So where's my hankie?" asked my mother. "Oh, I couldn't remember what I was supposed to fetch," I mumbled. "Well! You *are* a silly," said she, getting up and putting the book down on her chair, "I'll get it myself."

GYPSIES

Each year until the war began, or perhaps even the first year of the war too, Spring brought the Peg-Lady, my mother's friend. Her visits were as regular, and as reassuring, as the first sight of swallows in northern skies. She was a Romany, not a tinker; and she brought the wooden clothes-pegs—the doll-like kind with a little rounded head and two legs, not the kind with a metal spring—which her family whittled in the winter months (wherever they spent them, which my mother knew but I never heard or thought to ask about). And her son came with her—a chair caner. Our dining room chairs had seats woven of some kind of fiber—not cane—and also we had four cane chairs, including the "littlest Bear" chair from my earliest childhood; so there was sometimes some repair work for him at our house; and if not, at one or another of the houses in our street of two long blocks. If there were a chair to be caned, he took it out onto the clean, wide pavement (sidewalk, Americans would say) beyond the front garden and sat there peacefully busy, the work held between his outstretched legs. (It was not until after World War II that parked cars began to clutter such residential streets; little traffic passed in the roadway.) His mother, the Peg-

Lady, meanwhile went from house to house with her basket, selling her wares and obtaining orders for him. At our house she spent a long time, for my mother always asked her in, made tea for her, offered her a snack. They would sit at the kitchen table, face to face, and she would recount her news of the year—the deaths and births and marriages of her numerous relations, her wanderings since the previous spring. Later my mother always seemed to glow as if elated. She would tell us (my father and sister and I) something of the conversation when we were gathered at the next meal—the one o'clock dinner if the gypsies had come in the morning, as they usually did, or at supper that evening if they had not come till afternoon; but somehow, when I got old enough to think of it at all, I always perceived her friendship with the Peg-Lady as a private matter, and some instinct, even years later, stopped me from asking questions about what they said to each other beyond the simple exchange of news. I'm certain, though, that it was not a matter of her telling fortunes, for if it had been there would have been a sense of anxiety associated with her visits; and in time my mother would have confided something of her predictions, as she did about another gypsy encounter. Something lay behind her considering the Peg-Lady as a friend; an incident which seemed to me to be part of a remote historical past, but which, when I count the years backward, had really happened only about eighteen years before I first heard it recounted.

At that time my parents—engaged but not yet married and therefore travelling with a chaperone—were *en route* by boat from Constantinople to Venice, via Athens. A large party of Balkan gypsies was on board—wealthy gypsies, as could be seen from their gorgeous embroidered clothing, the great strings of gold and silver coins worn by the womenfolk as necklaces, the gold and silver braid on the men's waist-coats. All—men, women, and children—were of proud and even fierce bearing; many were strikingly handsome. They flashed about the deck like birds of paradise. But something was wrong: one among them was very sick and needed some kind of help or medicine, and the captain of the ship could not (or would not?) understand. My father was an excellent linguist and intervened in their behalf, talking with them in whichever Slavic language they spoke, and with the Captain in Turkish. Whatever it was that they required was given to the invalid. My mother could understand little if any of what was said but her face expressed sympathy and interest as she looked back and forth from my father to the gypsy spokesman. As the ship made its way along the Illyrian coast, it approached a tiny port where it was not scheduled to call. The little harbor, with its fishing boats, its tall narrow houses, backed by the mountains that rose beyond a strip of coastal flatland, came slowly into focus; and then it could be perceived that on the quay a small crowd of gypsies was waiting, some on horseback, some holding riderless horses or standing by the shafts of wagons. Amidst noise, confusion, and general excitement, but nevertheless with superb dignity, the party of gypsies from the boat disembarked, to be received with pomp and circumstance by those who waited—watched by the idlers, children, and fisherfolk of the little town and by the crew and passengers of the vessel. While the ship slowly put out to sea again, bales and bundles, a chest or two, were quickly stowed in the baggage-wagons; children and old folk (including the venerable invalid) along with some of the women, were established in other carts. The gypsies were still clearly visible to my parents, watching by the ship's rail, when the rest mounted their horses—some boys and girls and young women riding tandem. The whole caravan moved off in a cloud of golden dust and was soon no longer perceptible. But my mother retained not only the vivid memory of what she had seen, which she passed on to me so that it became my memory too in some measure; she had also been given a promise. This promise was, indeed, given as much to my father as to her, but it was alien to him and he gave it no credence; it became her possession because she cherished it.

What had happened was that, before going down the companionway, the chief of the whole group—tall, moustachioed, jacket aglitter with silver braid—came to my parents and said that the old man who was ill was the Gypsy King, and that, because of their help on this voyage, gypsies anywhere, in any place in the world, would be grateful and would consider them as benefactors; it would be necessary only to describe the event, and any Romany would be at once at their service. As I have said, my father did not take this seriously. But my mother, throughout the rest of her life, would tell the tale to any gypsies she met, and it was always honored. The most persistent Romany saleswoman or beggar, as soon as she heard it, would cease her pitch.

I witnessed the most dramatic of such encounters when I was seven. We were in Wales, in Merionethshire, for the summer holidays, and most days the four of us—parents and two girls—took long walks, even ascending Cader Idris on one occasion. This was the loveliest mountain country—heath and heather, sheep-cropped turf with its many tiny wildflowers, larks rising, glimpses of shining sea to the West. My mother was deeply content in such surroundings; though this particular part of Wales was new to her, it was her native land and her own best-loved kind of landscape. She would sing as we walked sometimes—or make me get the giggles by bleating at the sheep with such authenticity that they never failed to respond, and a dialogue in sheep-language would ensue. My father shed his clerical collar and walked jacketless in the sunshine with his shirtsleeves rolled up, and joked with us.

One day, as our footpath led over a rise, we came upon a tall gypsy woman striding towards us. She had a large basket over her arm, and looked, I thought, just like Meg Merrilies (for I loved that poem). At once she broke into the usual pleading whine about "cross my hand with silver and I'll tell your fortune, my lady," and began, too, to display the contents of her basket—bits of lace and lengths of ribbon. But my mother with equal promptitude began to tell about the royal gypsies of the Adriatic journey and the gratitude of the Gypsy King, while my father, embarrassed by the retelling of this

tale, so familiar to him, pursued the conversation he
was having with my fifteen-year-old sister, the apple of
his eye. They moved out of earshot together. I hung
about, half listening to both conversations but distract-
ed by a thousand other interesting things—the sheep
grazing among the gorse bushes and wild thyme, the
buzzing of bees, cloud and sunshine stirring on the
mountains. But I did register the gypsy's changed
demeanor when she had heard about the royal promise.
Facing her quietly, she took my mother's hand and
looked her in the eye. Then she began to talk softly to
her in a voice stripped of cajolery. She was telling her
fortune—at first in an ordinary predictable way, it
seems (for now my source is not my own perceptions
but what my mother recounted later, grafted onto my
own memory). But when she caught sight of my sister a
second change came over her; the tone and manner, at
first that of a habitual beggar or insistent saleswoman,
and then intimate and undemanding, was now, after a
moment's startled pause, even more markedly trans-
formed: drawing a deep breath, she began to prophesy.
It was a lower voice that sounded now; not loud, even a
little hoarse, but penetrating and turbulently fast. Her
hold on my mother's hand tightened, she looked
through her, not at her, as she told of many troubles
that were coming to my sister, many troubles brought
by her to my parents. My mother was terrified by the
sense that the gypsy could really see something beyond
the present, the impression that she was in the grip of a
speech that, though it was intelligible English, was akin
to echolalia in its swift involuntary flow; and by the

fierceness of that strong hand. But she stood firm and made no movement away from the gypsy; indeed she was transfixed by her power, or the power—the second sight—that charged her. Second sight was a phenomenon she had never doubted, for the dearest person in her life as a child—her step-aunt Helen—had had it. Suddenly the flow of speech ended; the gypsy's hand relaxed; her eyes now looked pityingly at my mother, and over at my father and sister, and at me too, though by then I was away in the heather pursuing a bleating lamb I longed to touch and tame.

By the time I'd run back, all three of my family were gathered round amiably saying goodbye to her and preparing to resume the walk. My mother smiled and chatted as if nothing especially dramatic, certainly nothing troubling, had occurred. The holiday's serenity was not disturbed. I joined in the farewells, and the gypsy reached into her large round basket and fished out a bit of silk lace and gave it to me. It was a cheap machine-made lace, but a romantic treasure to me, and I kept it for decades. She had already given some trinkets to my mother and sister. No money was offered or taken—the story of royal patronage had done its work. My mother said she'd made some predictions, but what she recounted to us was trivial. "What did she say about *me?*" I wanted to know; but was informed I was too young to have a fortune.

Whatever it was that had been predicted, my mother never told my sister about it, and never, even long after, told its specifics to my father and me either. Perhaps it was not detailed, but only a perception of misfortune and suffering. But many years later, when my sister was dead, my mother, a very old lady living in Mexico, would still speak of that meeting, and of how she had tried to convince herself it was nonsense and superstition; and how there still were happy times after that for a while; but that during the turbulence which soon began and was to mark the rest of my sister's life, she would often hear again the gypsy's voice and see her look, and feel again, in memory, her warm, callused, powerful hand.

BY THE SEASIDE

Clacton. Clacton. Not a pleasant sound. But it has a color: the yellowish beige of sand. I see myself and my mother and sister shaking sand out of our shoes at the top of one of the flights of steps leading from the beach to the Promenade, or was it called the Parade . . . . Midday, dinnertime, and we are returning to our lodgings a few blocks from the Front for one of those meat and two veg meals which give to English lodgings the classic smell of cabbage.

Miss Ware's. Were there other lodgers? I remember none. Of Miss Ware herself I have only an impression of amiability, a toothy smile, animated conversation. Our room was crowded with beds, looming wardrobe, tall chest of drawers, washstand with china bowl and pitcher and slop pail beneath; and its predominating tones were dark greens and browns resembling the seaweed I kept bringing back from the beach. You could predict the next day's weather: the seaweed stayed slippery, there would be rain, or turned brittle so that you could pop the bubbles in it, and next day would be sunny. No matter that we shook our shoes out each time we left the beach, there was always sand on the carpet and between the sheets. I liked the feel of that.

I would wander away from our daily beach encampment of rug, towels, and books. What drew me especially was a rambling path along the grass at the top of the cliffs. I am not sure there *are* any cliffs at Clacton; certainly no very high ones. But even if this path led along the top of mere dunes, they were cliffs to me; and what I liked were some shallow caves the path skirted. Boys must have dug them by enlarging disused rabbit holes; and possibly lovers sheltered in them after dusk. But I considered them genuine and romantic caves, and planned to conceal some necessities of adventure in the deepest one: supplies, such as a tin of biscuits, my pocket compass, a treasure map; and to make it my own secret camp. The pleasure was to imagine myself sitting in it, scanning the ocean with a spyglass; it was not necessary to *do* it. I had read more than once the beginning of a tale (meant for older girls, and boring after the first chapter) in which a girl had discovered a cave, a much bigger, rockier one, to which she alone knew the secret path, and from its opening used to watch the sailboats and liners and cargo steamers in the wide expanse of Sydney Harbor . . . a scene I saw myself many decades later.

My sister, who would have been sixteen or seventeen at the time, was strong willed and persuasive. My mother must, that summer, have been under her spell, for she let Olga drill me for hours every day on the beach, in preparation for taking a ballet exam. This exam was of no concern to me (except as Olga urged me towards it) and indeed I had no clear idea of what it would be like to take any exam, since I didn't go to school but "did lessons" at home. And whether or not I became particularly proficient in dancing was certainly not of concern to our mother. However, it was for the moment Olga's obsession; and so each day she put me through my paces—"*barre*" for which some wall or stair-railing was used in lieu of an actual bar; "floor-work"—*attitudes* and *arabesques* and *port de bras;* and "elevation" (which was what I liked best, the *jetés* and *grand jetés* and other leaps and bounds).

My mother sat on the sand, her back against the promenade wall, knitting, reading, or just gazing out to sea, watching clouds and the play of light and shadow as she loved to do; and Olga, with all her phenomenal energy and dedication, shouted and counted and made up *enchainements* and urged me beyond my natural capacities and inclinations. I would get cross or even tearful at times; but though I had my moments of being *fed-up,* I didn't really hate all this. Olga could scold fiercely but she always flattered as well, so that my self-esteem was reinforced; and I really did love the sense of having graceful arms and strong "elevation." Since I was a solitary child for the most part, who did not participate in any athletics, it was no doubt a good release of animal spirits.

One day, around the time of sunset, when my practice was over, I noticed that my mother and sister, busy with picking up our beach paraphernalia preparatory to returning to Miss Ware's, were conversing with a lady and gentleman who were leaning down over the parapet of the promenade. Uninterested, I took the opportunity to slip down to the water's edge just one more time. The tide was ebbing, and the sand which the waves had just left and were still returning to with last calm kisses, was glistening. The sun had vanished, but the sky deepened its pink and gold, which each turning wave reflected before absorbing them into its green; and each wave was briefly reflected in the wet sand. A small wind lifted my hair—and without any thought for Olga, or exams, or the correct way to hold my fingers (in the stiff English "operatic" ballet convention then prevailing), I began to dance for myself, for the afterglow and the *hush: hush:* of the sea receding. Dancing lessons had not been *my* idea, but Olga had had her way, and it now proved after all to be a gift to me, however complex her motives (which included a strange need for vicarious success). At that moment, on that smooth and hard-packed sand, whatever was dubious and self-interested about her fanatical coaching was of no importance: she had enabled me to express the ecstasy I felt. I leapt, I glided, I twirled, I invented steps and used my whole sturdy seven-year-old body to be at one with the luminous and now fading sky, the soft air, the farewelling of the waves. Then my mother was calling me and I was trudging back over the softer dry sand towards her and Olga, to go home for high tea, and reading aloud, and eventually bedtime.

I had unwittingly saved what could have been a most distressing situation for them. The people who'd stopped to talk had not done so accidentally: they were concerned for my welfare and had accused my mother of letting my sister torture me, making me practice from morning to night and not play like other children. They had been ready to report my case to the Royal Society for the Prevention of Cruelty to Children. With what astonishment they witnessed my unselfconscious and clearly voluntary performance! Convinced of their error, they had departed apologetically.

Clacton held another ecstasy for me. I slipped out again by myself after tea, another day, for a last look at the waves. While I was running along by the sea wall, along came the lamplighter on his bicycle, with his long lighting-stick: for some reason parts of the town were still lit by gas well into the 1930's. He was heading inland, riding slowly along, pausing at each lamppost to touch it awake. I began to lope behind him at a respectful distance. He was not just a lamplighter, he embodied the mystique of Robert Louis Stevenson's "Leerie," with all the added depth of drama Charles Robinson's black-and-white drawings gave to the simplest words in my edition of *A Child's Garden of Verses*. I had run down Miss Ware's street towards the sea while it was still daylight, but now with each lamp he kindled, everything outside its immediate circle darkened, though the lofty sky still held its pallor: street by street and lamppost by lamppost he led on, paying no heed to me, perhaps unaware a child was following.

At last I found myself many streets away from our lodgings—streets empty of people or traffic of any kind, and beyond all sound of the sea. Curtains were drawn over the windows of silent houses. I was barefoot, and could feel the warmth still held in the smooth paving. In the twilight I could make out the occasional squares of cement that were pink instead of grey—the special ones I liked.

I was quite alone; he had lit his last lamp and speeded away. But I felt only the faintest stir of anxiety—just enough to turn me round to patter silently back to where I could sense, and presently begin to hear, the sea again. I found Miss Ware's street without trouble; and my mother and Olga were cheerfully gossiping with her. My absence for so much longer than was intended had not been noticed. It was probably not very long at all in clock time, although it seemed to me that I was returning from a far place. I had witnessed, in conscious solitude, that magical transformation, *entre chien et loup,* which Magritte has evoked in certain paintings. The lamplighter, invested with mythic power, had with his wand performed an alchemy upon both light and darkness.

But alas, Clacton's associations are not all of high moments. At the end of our ten-day visit my father came down from London to fetch us, and we all went walking along the shore to Frinton. Frinton really does have cliffs, and we took a path that led along their grassy verge. Running back and forth, ahead and around the grown-ups like a dog, I kept going close to the edge, and my parents kept calling out to me not to do so. My father had a fear of heights, a fear that became doubly keen when he saw his own child at the edge of a considerable drop. Showing off, and scornful of his dismay, I persisted. It spoiled the walk for him (and ultimately for me too, for I hated to be in disgrace, and especially couldn't bear my mother's infrequent anger for long). When I grew up and had a child of my own, I felt all that my father had felt. How I exasperated my son with my dread of heights and narrow ledges where he wanted to clamber! The sight of any child, though a total stranger to me, running too close to such an edge makes me flinch. I once, perhaps two years before the Clacton incident, ruined a trip with my father on a day steamer by insisting on running around the decks and clambering on the side-rails. I never would have dared to tease my mother like that—indeed I never had the slightest impulse to do so. But my father, gentle and somewhat solemn, stirred a provocative and most unpleasant devil in me.

I wonder if he remembered that day—either of those days—with a shudder, long after, as I did? Or whether despite the moments of painful anxiety I gave him, he recalled quite other things?—the pleasure of rejoining his family, the salty air he always enjoyed so much, the gulls wheeling and crying in the sea light? Thoughts, hopes, loves, sorrows. He may, recalling Clacton, have collaged its images with memories of the Baltic or the Bosphorus. What vast and solitary labyrinths, crowded with oceans, with shells and shards, room corners and fleeting smiles, with cities and intentions, each of us encloses!

TWO ANCIENTS

The church of which my father had been appointed Priest-in-Charge had been built to serve a Dickensian, "thieves kitchen" population in that part of the East End of London described by the Victorian novelist Arthur Morison in *Children of the Jago;* but slum clearance by the Baroness Burdett Coutts and others, who put up solidly-built massive tenements of a kind still to be seen in some parts of London, and usually referred to as "the Buildings," in the same way that in the U.S. people call subsidized high-rise developments "the Projects," had changed the character of the neighborhood. By the 1920's it was solidly respectable Jewish immigrant working class. Consequently there was virtually no congregation to attend services in the rather beautiful but somber sanctuary, which had been constructed on the upper floor, while the ground floor had originally been intended—and used—as a men's shelter and soup kitchen. There was no vicarage, only a flat, which in my childhood was occupied by our former maid Amy; when she married and stopped working for us, she and her husband were installed there as caretakers.

Sometimes my mother and sister and I, with Amy

and her husband and child, were virtually the only per-
sons at the weekly service at Holy Trinity (though my
father's scholarship and his eloquent preaching drew
large congregations at other churches, in Bloomsbury
and in Golders Green, with which he was then and later
connected). One who faithfully attended, however, was
an old man known in our family as The Spiritualist. I
was too young and shy to converse with him but I had a
kind of fondness for him. He looked so frail and deli-
cate—and I must have absorbed from my parents a
sense of tender concern for him. He was a small man,
small-boned, with small hands and feet, softly curling
shoulder-length white hair, and a little beard. One might
picture Henry James's Hyacinth, in *The Princess
Casamassima,* looking so had he lived to grow old. His
manner was extremely gentle. I believe he was all alone
in the world, having lost first his wife, then a beloved
daughter. He had been a printer, and now lived on the
Old Age pittance of the period. To please him, a hymn
he had at some point earnestly requested was sung every
week if he were present—"Living Water." I think it
must have been a revivalist hymn, and was certainly not
included in *The Church Hymnal,* which was what we
used, and perhaps not even in the less high-church
Hymns Ancient and Modern—it was handed out on a
separate mimeographed sheet. But there was something
powerful in the sight and sound of the old man fervent-
ly singing in his quavery, reedy voice the words he
loved, "Living water, living water," and when I think of
him I not only see the dark, candlelit church (which
gave off a certain stony chill even in warm weather, a

chill that contrasted tantalizingly with the sensuous per-
fume of incense), but also glimpse a green pasture with
a sparkling fountain at its center.

He is linked inextricably to another figure I recall.
From time to time an old man would appear in our sub-
urban street with a barrel-organ, which was no more
than a large superannuated music box balanced precari-
ously on a fragile old perambulator. This old man
seemed to me even then to resemble The Spiritualist,
and now their appearance is identical in my memory,
except that the organ-grinder wears a battered hat and a
long coat (which evoked for me the nursery rhyme
about "Old Grimes"—who "used to wear a long brown
coat/All buttoned down before"). He seemed so feeble
that he could scarcely push the creaking pram, whose
thin-rimmed wheels wobbled as it went. He would
come to a halt in the middle of the street (there was vir-
tually no traffic in those days) and begin to turn the
handle of his music box. It had only one tune, and in
the several years of his sporadic but not infrequent
appearances, it lost more and more notes and got more
and more out of tune; but it had a melancholy charm I
adored. A familiar passage in *Petrouchka* gives one an
idea of it—or even more so, Stravinsky's *Suite* for
Chamber Orchestra; a wheezy, broken-winded, yet inef-
fably romantic sound, summoning up a blended pathos
and irony my childish mind had no words for but which
gave me acute pleasure.

What is strange is that my kind mother never, as far
as I know, sent him out a penny, nor did I think of
demanding to do so; and I can't remember seeing any of

our neighbors give him anything either. I watched him from my upstairs window where I was supposed to be "doing my lessons," and he never looked up, or seemed to glance towards the houses at all. After feebly turning the handle for a while—slower and slower as his arm tired—he let the music tinkle and tweedle to a stop, and then slowly shuffled off, pushing the pram dejectedly as if he'd had no expectations of receiving anything anyway.

If something causes me to recall one of them, I always think also of the other ancient, frail, solitary man. Yet how different the two!—one was an image of despondency (though his music's charm gave off some faint sense of a world of gaiety long past, a gaiety tinged with melancholy, that delicate bittersweet mood I was later to recognize in Watteau's *fêtes*); while the other, in gentle fervor, testified to a faith and joy that seemed to negate his decrepitude.

A DANCE

The Courtwells' house, number seven, is architecturally identical to ours, number five, but inside it is a different world. They have few books, while in our house, only the bathroom and lavatory are without crammed bookshelves. And the Courtwells sit in their dining room and kitchen, using their drawing room only for special occasions. Our drawing room—the long room with bay windows looking onto the front garden and street and with French windows at the other end looking onto the back garden—is in full use. Mr. Courtwell is gone to his business all day, with his oldest son; the younger son and grown-up daughter are often gone, too. But in our house it seems as if we are all at home most of the time. At least one person is almost always in the drawing room, reading or writing, practicing the piano, drawing, listening to the radio; sometimes all of us, my father, mother, sister and I, anyone who happens to be staying with us for a while—a German student, a Welsh cousin up to take the London Matric exams—are there together and very likely all talking at once. It is a busy room, lined with books, with two sofas near the fireplace as well as armchairs; there are other chairs also, and small tables, desks, sewing materials. It's where my mother

teaches me my lessons in the mornings, and reads aloud
to all of us in the evenings.

Margaret Courtwell, who is two or three years older
than I, is my friend, but it's not just so we can play
together that she comes to our house whenever she can:
the books, and all that she overhears, fascinate her,
though she never says a word in the midst of it. There
are curtains framing the drawingroom windows, but no
venetian blinds; during the day the light comes first
from the bay windows and later, aslant, from the garden
doors, picking out objects of polished brass or my sis-
ter's bright knitting wools. For most months of the year
there's a glowing coal fire in the hearth too. Our draw-
ing room is alive all the time.

But though the Courtwells' house has its own busy
life, with her mother's church work and many charities,
her two teen-age brothers and her sister, even older than
my big sister, and her sister's beaux, their drawing room
is in a trance. The blinds are down, only a subaqueous
light filters in upon the white-shrouded furniture. The
carpet is rolled up and encased in white drugget. It is a
place of silence and mystery. It fascinates me as keenly
as ours does Margaret.

Into that silence Margaret and I, some days when I
go next door to play, are permitted to enter. Usually it's
on a day when it is too wet, too hot or too cold, for
outdoor play. Often no one but Bertha, the Courtwell's
chubby maid who comes from Mrs. Courtwell's Kentish
village birthplace (and who, my mother says, rules their
household), is home on the days when we are allowed
to play in their drawing room. Bertha knows we will be

absorbed for a long time and give no trouble in there. There is nothing to break, for the bric-a-brac is put away and only brought out on the rare occasions when the furniture is unshrouded, the carpet unrolled.

What lures us into the dim and melancholy room, a room in which we feel at first compelled to whisper, is the piano. It's a player piano. And what we do in there is take turns, one dancing while the other pedals away, watching over her shoulder the dancer's dreamy movements.

Both of us have taken lessons down the street at Miss Lawrence's classes: ballet, "Greek," "acrobatic," and tap. But these private dancings scarcely draw on any of that—unless, perhaps, a little on the relative freedom of "Greek." What we do—though it is years before I find a word for it—is a spontaneous eurythmy. The music on the rolls, what is it? Old overtures, waltzes, palm court czardas . . . .

We don't talk much, never criticize each other's performance, lend—as each takes her turn at the piano bench—grave assent to the leaps and whirls we watch, the flailing of arms in storm, the outstretched imploring hands, the solemn pacing in unspecified situations of delay and decision, or the twittering feet of surprise and delight as the music hops into cheerful briskness. We never laugh at one another. We don't verbalize our responses to the music, so I never learn what Margaret has in mind; but I know that what happens for me is a drama of unspecified Loss, Discovery, Flight, *Sehnsucht,* ecstatic Joy, Danger . . . . No definite story, no named persons, no clear dilemmas, but the sweeping passage of grand emotions. A very few years later, when I am ten and see Salvator Rosa's dark landscapes, illuminated by bursts of sunlight and thronged by bandits and mysterious travelers, I see that they correspond closely to what I experienced in my improvisations to the Courtwells' player piano rolls.

The afternoon (it is always afternoon) begins to darken towards teatime; between the slats of the venetian blinds filters a paleness that tells of clearing skies after a day of rain. Soon Bertha will call us both to tea or my mother will send for me to come home. But there is an external present where, alternately, Margaret and I, aged forever nine and seven, waltz, and whirl, and strike poses among the ghostly loomings of white-draped settees and ottomans, held in the vague greenish stare of a gilt-framed over-mantel looking glass.

THE GARDENER

Very tall, very pale, a man of bone and mist, he moves up and down our street in all seasons, stopping now at one house, now at another. It is Old Day, the gardener, and half the householders in the block employ him. The brick houses, connected by party walls, are all alike except that a few, at our end of the street, are wider by an additional room at the kitchen end, and thus have two entrances. All have front gardens, each with its familiar character—a dusty gloom of ground-ivy or a blaze of flowers; and each flower garden specializes: some can be counted on for roses, some for dahlias. My mother's, in midsummer, is golden with California poppies. Here and there a laburnum or a red maytree leans out toward the passerby from behind the low iron railings that surround each front garden.

But behind every house is the far larger back garden, wholly invisible from the street, and only partly visible even to next-door neighbors (including those on the parallel street whose gardens are back-to-back with ours), for they are separated from one another with brick walls as tall as a grown person, and often a further privacy has been given by well-grown trees or lilac bushes planted along their three sides. If, from our own,

I look down the line of back gardens, I see what seems to be a narrow forest. Standing on a wooden crate placed close to one of our side walls, I can look directly into Foxes' on the left, or I can move it over to see Courtwells' on the right; or, over the back wall, a bit of Burnes's garden and Mrs. Peach's (for those next-street houses are not exactly aligned with ours). Those four, then, are known. All other gardens, all the way down the street, are secrets. But Old Day knows every secret, must have seen even those in which he hasn't worked, and even what lies behind the houses on the far side of the street. He walks through the houses and out into the hidden squares. Do all have lawns? Do some have gold-fish pools, shrubberies, arbors? In ours there is a rockery made of dark, porous cindery stuff—tufa, perhaps. And the Courtwells have a rockery of smooth white rocks which, when Margaret Courtwell and I rub our hands on them, give off a magical silver dust.

Bone and mist, deliberate, sardonic in his silence, he tends and he destroys. My mother transplants some wild primroses from a distant hedgerow where she dug them up on a day in the country. She shows them to Old Day and firmly warns him against injuring them when he weeds the beds. He digs them up. This happens again, with other treasures. Each time she cries with disappointment and anger, swears she will not hire him again. But after a while he is back. He is capable of helping as well as of hindering.

One time a crew of Irishmen come to make a new lawn. My sister's Drama Society has rehearsed in the garden all summer and trampled the grass to death. So it is to be dug and turved. The men carrying loads of new-cut slabs of turf pass back and forth from their horse and cart parked in the street, tramp through the kitchen gate, the front garden, the kitchen door, the kitchen, down a step into the scullery, out into the trellis-screened, paved utility yard, and into the garden. Kitchen and scullery smell of earth and new grass. The men shout to each other in a fine brogue. Old Day is there, watching, impassive. He has been told not to let them dig up my special daisy, one whose petals are tipped with red, which grows—wild, but cared for—at the corner of the grassplot, by the base of an iron post up which a climbing rose is trained, near the French windows of our drawing room. They have been told, he has been told; but they forget, and he watches and says not a word as a spade goes into that corner, cuts into the daisy's roots, turns the plant under into the soil.

The Courtwells, the Burneses, whose gardens are tidier than ours and less abundant, have fewer problems with him. It is the abundance of our garden, my mother's inclusive and generous style of horticulture, that he seems to punish. In my copy of *Parables from Nature* there is an engraving that shows Old Day. I have never read the story; most of the pictures in this book have, in fact, a life quite independent of the texts to which they are attached; but I can see well enough that he is a person of ancient power; indeed, an embodiment of Time—have I not heard the phrase, Old Father Time?—or of Death. In the engraving there are two representations of him: one shows him leaning forward to examine the inscription on a sundial; this figure wears a sort of sou'wester hat, and carries under his arm a telescope for looking into past and future. The sundial stands in a churchyard crowded with antique tombstones, leaning this way and that. In the lower right-hand part of the picture he is shown digging a grave. He's right down in the grave, shovelling out the dirt with the same spade he used to bury my mother's primroses. His white hair sticks out below the brim of his hat, and there's a pleasant smile on his face. "Active and Passive," is the caption beneath the engraving.

My mother claims Old Day is stupid as well as malevolent; but though she employed another gardener once, for a few months, in the end she took Day back. His imperturbable persistence is equivalent to reliability, and at least he wastes no time talking. And I, though he rarely says a word to me, and though I know he is a dark power, and though there is something alarming in the mild, complacent pleasantness of his expression as, in that dark engraving, he shovels out a deep hole for someone dead to lie in—I nevertheless have a secret liking for him.

I grow up, some houses are destroyed by bombs in the blitz, I'm away working as a hospital nurse, the war claims all the iron railings from the front gardens, the war ends, I marry and cross the ocean. Old Day asks after me. My mother is amazed.

Years later, our house long since bought by strangers, I revisit the street, note what has changed, what is unchanged, nod to the sinister laurel bush near our kitchen window. A long-ago neighbor tells me Old Day must have died, she thinks. "Yes," I say, "he was white-haired when I was a young child, and seemed even then like a walking skeleton; yes, I suppose he can't still be alive." But I know better. Bone and mist, pale, white-haired, grey-eyed, very tall, clothed in colors of ash and earth, a capricious demigod, he still moves in a stately shamble up and down the block, glides unobserved right through certain houses, brings life and blossom, death and burial to the rectangular sanctums closed off from each other by walls of brick and thickets of may, laburnum, apple trees, memory, time. He carries sometimes a spade, sometimes a scythe, and listens in silence to orders he will not obey. He has his own intentions.

JANUS

Moments of childhood lodge in one's memory sometimes for reasons—their beauty, drama, or comedy; others equally tenacious are unaccountable: why that instant rather than a million others? One that has for me both beauty and drama has been slow to reveal a further dimension I now perceive. I wonder if Trixie remembers it too, or Jean Pilgrim, assuming they're still alive?

Beautiful Trixie Burnes lived on the next street and her back garden partially adjoined ours. What wonderful cartwheels and handsprings she turned, round and round the Burnes's lawn! We played together sometimes, ranging glass jars on top of the brick wall between our gardens and filling them with flower petals and water, trying to produce perfume or magic potions (until they rotted and stank). Or we pushed doll's prams down York Road to a secret path that led through bramble bushes to the muddy banks of the Roding. But Trixie, a couple of years older than I, went to the Convent School and had a whole other life with other friends, and there were long periods when she was not available. I knew only one of these school friends of hers, and even with her had only the scantest acquaintance; but I admired the idea of her, which seemed to have a certain aura, a glamour. Perhaps it had to do with the attractive sound of her name, Jean Pilgrim; and with the fact that she had initiated a game called "Murder" at Trixie's birthday party (so Trixie told me) which apparently was an elaborate kind of hide-and-seek, all over the house, nowhere out of bounds.

This one day of the adventure which I remember at least once a year was the only time I went anywhere outside our own gardens with Trixie, except down to the river with our dolls, and the only time without exception that I played with any of her school friends. I had met the group of them—Trixie, Jean and one or two others—as they were coming home from the Convent and I was coming from the Park on my scooter (my home lessons were done long before other children's school hours were over). In the Cranbrook Road not far from the gates of Valentines Park stood one of the last large Victorian houses, remnant of the village which the flooding tide of London had not many years before reached and engulfed, transforming it into the growing suburb it now was. Shuttered and boarded up for a long time, the broad, three-storey, grey brick, slate-roofed mansion was meant for a large family and plenty of servants. Many such houses, all over England, were torn down, as this would be, in the '20s and '30s when servants were scarce, families smaller, and a generation of sons had been killed off in the trenches. (Others, still standing after WWII, would be saved by conversion into warrens of flats.) Behind this looming structure, which, of course, because it was empty, we

readily invested with a ghost, and would have been ter-
rified to enter, extended a large square plot of ground
surrounded by an unusually high brick wall. And Jean
Pilgrim, as we stood gathered in the street, suddenly
suggested that we climb the wall and explore the secret
garden it must hide.

Outside of back-garden play with Trixie or with
Margaret-next-door (who now had gone away to
boarding-school anyway), most of my adventures were
solitary; and the prospect of this exploit with a group of
older girls was thrillingly like something children did in
books. Whispering, giggling, excited, we made our way
(I don't recall how) between the side of the empty house
and the business neighboring it, and looked for a place
in the high enclosing wall that might offer a foothold.
There seemed to be none; but with some difficulty,
standing on one another's shoulders, clawing the bricks,
grabbing legs or arms, heaving ourselves up, we did get
to the top and cling there, wall-edge pressing against
chests, to look over and in. And our surreptitious
squealing and out-of-breath chatter abruptly stopped.

For what we saw came out of a fairytale or a poem:
a tree of medium height but wide-spreading, concealed
till now by those towering walls, and covered in huge
white blossoms bigger than tulips, waxy, perfect; a tree
such as none of us had ever seen. I know that I, anyway,
had never even heard of a magnolia. Its leaves were
dark glossy green, those white flowers were whiter than
white, glowing with transcendent beauty. If any of the
brown stain which so quickly defaces magnolia blossom
were present, it went unseen. The silence this ecstatic

vision imposed on us all for that long moment makes me believe our response was fully collective.

There was nothing else in the square of garden—just the shaggy remains of a lawn, and a gravel path round it, and the overgrown flowerbeds. No color but green, and in its midst the tree.

Then our shrill, excited voices came back, exclaiming—and no sooner had they done so than, oh, terror! An old tramp burst out of the house, hairy, purple-faced, shouting at us, waving a stick! With shrieks we dropped back down, scraping hands and knees, landing with a shock in a momentary scramble of bodies, to pick ourselves up with scared swiftness and race back to the safety of the street. The devil in paradise! A live tramp in the house was more terrifying than ghosts.

That's the little drama I remember each year when I see a magnolia tree in full bloom (or in Boston a whole vista of them in Commonwealth Avenue's center strip). Enough in itself—especially as the association with that shadowy, somehow elfin figure, Jean Pilgrim (of whose exact appearance I have no image, only a sense of someone wiry, narrow-faced in an attractive way, curly-haired, daring), lends it an extra element, a feeling of *story,* as if it had been an episode in some children's mystery-tale, the rest of which was missing. But now, more than sixty years later, I see that there may have been, all along, another reason for the persistent recurrence of this memory. Wasn't it one of the earliest intimations of how close to one another are beauty and terror, how intimately related? The tree in full splendor, enclosed in its walled garden, its *temenos,* hidden. . . .

Our sight of it an epiphany, a glimpse of unearthly beauty (or rather, of an earthly beauty beyond all expectation). And at that precise instant, the raging monster exploding from the long-closed mansion where none but ghosts were supposed to be, our hearts jumping almost out of our bodies (though in reality he may have been merely a poor old squatter, or even—it's just possible—an appointed caretaker). We had scaled a wall, trespassing; by forbidden means we had partaken of a glory not ours to taste; and though no god transformed us from human children to stags or some other life-form, we had to pay for our transgression: is that it? But no, it's not transgression and retribution I read there, but—less simply, and with less sense of cause and effect—a revelation of how intimately opposites live, their mysterious simultaneity, their knife-edge union: the Janus face of human experience.

AN EARLY LOVE

Butov, the Gypsy singer, comes swiftly out of the stage door looking for Olga. I'm eight years old, cast as a go-between, poised in anxious readiness, primed to tell him Olga's looking for him in the "front-of-the-house." He sweeps me into a bear-hug, takes my hand, and we run down the alley together. This is my first taste of romance, although as we turn the corner she's there, seventeen and fiercely in love, and my one-line role has been played.

In the afternoon he arrives at our house, wearing a dark suit. He's not really a Gypsy, he's Russian, or maybe Bulgarian, thirty years old—I hear all this when my mother, later, is telling a friend. And he's come to ask, with complete propriety, for Olga's hand in marriage. Father, of course, kindly but firmly says no. They talk man to man in Russian. Butov bows to necessity, somberly departs. From my upstairs window I watch him shut the garden gate behind him and walk away, neither fast nor slow, his head down—back to the theater, the troupe, that night's show and the next day's train.

Where was Olga? I only remember my own regret, my dreams of writing to tell him—what? Of assuring him *I* was loyal, I would be glad if he tried again, I would be forever his friend, his messenger, his ally. . . . Those dreams lasted long after Olga's had turned to new suitors.

THE LAST OF CHILDHOOD
—FOR JEAN, IN THIS LIFE OR THE NEXT

Jean Rankin was the first friend I chose myself and who chose me, rather than a next-door neighbor or a child whose family my mother or sister knew. Jean and I met in the park, both gazing into a small but mesmeric waterfall. I was between nine and ten, she a year younger. Each of us immediately recognized a kindred spirit, and for almost two years we'd meet almost every weekday, as well as Saturday mornings. If something prevented it, we left notes for each other in a certain hole in the bank of the stream—our post-office. She had to cross the park four times a day on her way to and from school.

I'd never known another child who completely understood my "pretend games" and could make up her own as well. Jean and I formed a Secret Society (of two) called The Adventure Seekers. As the elder, I was the Captain; she was the Mate. We sailed grassy seas in the three-masted barque Emanuela (did Jean have a "fairycycle" or did we take turns on my protean, large, homemade scooter?—I can't recall). As Robin Hood and Little John we prowled through the fenced-off bits of woodland near the upper lake and its waterfall—the head of our stream—and taunted the lame park-keeper (the Sheriff of Nottingham) who shouted and waved his stick but could never catch up with us. Jean's secret ambition at that time was to someday climb the Matterhorn.

When Jean was ill and not allowed out for ten days (she was somewhat delicate, or considered so by her mother), I was quite miserable and at loose ends; I looked up all the poems addressed to, or referring to, "Bonnie Jean" in a big old nineteenth-century *Complete Poems of Robert Burns,* with steel engravings, which had turned up in one of the "lots" my father would buy at Sotheby's from time to time. Disconsolately I mumbled them to myself. There were a few references to the name Jean or Jeannie in my book of border ballads, too.

This delightful friendship with a child who was indeed unusually charming—sensitive, intelligent, imaginative, and a true original (for there was not in her background the rich stimulus of books and music and talk that mine provided)—was unmarred for those two years by any argument or quarrel between us. Yet it came to an abrupt end, brought about by my own intransigent pride and hardheartedness.

It happened on a Saturday morning. On weekdays we played in Valentines, the park near both our houses (though these were not, themselves, close to each other). But sometimes on Saturdays we'd go to the outskirts of Wanstead Park, a more ancient and romantic domain. The interior of Wanstead Park was the one place considered out-of-bounds: in the 1930's there was so little violence in England that an assault on a young girl, which had taken place there before we were born, caused our parents to believe it was too dangerous a place for children to go unaccompanied. But the prohibition didn't apply to the open field that formed a prelude to the park's real beginning. The small river Roding divided the field from the wooded interior of the park and was crossed by a "rustic" bridge—the kind with protective railings made of knotty interlacings of irregular branches. Paddling and splashing around in the shallow water, planning but never really building a dam, was the sort of thing we'd always enjoyed. But suddenly on this day Jean was reluctant to take off her shoes and socks and tuck her skirt into her knickers. I was astonished. What had come over her? In retrospect, I think that probably her mother had been lecturing her, not just as usual—exhorting her not to get wet and chilled and catch a cold—but perhaps, now that Jean was approaching the age to start attending the County School (eleven years old), had been preparing her for the advent of her first menstrual period. (But my own mother never fussed about wet feet, and I was a year older.) Anyway, to my dismay, Jean said that now we were older it was *not ladylike* to mess about in the stream.

I was indignant, and launched into a lecture. That concept of what was ladylike was absurd and narrow-minded, I said; the only kind of ladylikeness that had any value was to be honorable and chivalrous, like a Knight of the Round Table. My mother was not a "lady" in that stupid way, and when we were on holiday in the country she would scramble under barbed wire or through a gap in a hedge, and would take off her shoes to ford a stream like any sensible person. But she was a *real* lady, in the only worthwhile sense, because she was kind and proud and honorable. And so forth. I must have ended up by saying that if Jean didn't retract her silly announcement and take her shoes off and get into the stream I'd never speak to her again.

Jean looked miserable but stuck to her guns. Probable her mother had extracted a promise from her. How torn she must have been! When I saw that I had not prevailed, I grimly put my own shoes and socks back on and in passionate anger started back home, my heart beating a mile a minute. At the gates I glanced back and saw that Jean was following.

There were parallel streets, Wanstead Park Road and The Drive, leading to where our homeward paths would diverge. I took Wanstead Park. At each intersection I paused and looked toward The Drive; and each time, at the corresponding corner, there would be the small figure of Jean, looking stricken, and obviously longing for me to relent. I looked straight ahead again and went on to the next corner. There she would be again. How short the distance was, how easily I could have turned into any of these side-streets, and she would no doubt have gladly come halfway to meet me! But I believed it was a matter of principle and wouldn't give an inch. I hardened my heart and went on—and at last we had passed the point where her road no longer lay parallel to mine, and the long desolate continuation of Wanstead Park Road lay before me, and I went home.

After a week or ten days Mrs. Rankin telephoned

and told me Jean missed me so much, and what was the matter, and would I not make friends? I forget what I said but in any case I refused to explain or relent. I too was sad and lonely, but my pride and the conviction I had about what constituted decent behavior overrode any impulse to give way. And it was years before I met Jean again.

This episode has been, throughout my adult life, a matter of shame and regret to me. I don't deplore my "lecture" in itself. "When Adam delved and Eve span, who was then the gentleman?" was in itself a worthy theme. But my unkindness and hardness of heart are a source of just remorse.

I wonder what would have happened to our friendship if the incident had not occurred? Each of us was on the threshold of change. Jean had passed the entrance exam for the County School and was soon to be caught up in a life very different from that of her Elementary School. And at the same time my sister would vigorously nudge and manipulate me into the new world of ballet school, where I would become as preoccupied with the love of dance as I had been with pretend-games and knights-errant and Robin Hood and happily messing about in muddy streams. Would our relationship have survived our new experiences? Even if it had not, it would presumably have diminished gradually and painlessly, not as a rupture that caused me, and very likely Jean too, abiding grief.

During the War, when we were about nineteen and twenty, we met again, but only briefly. Jean was a student at the London School of Economics and had fallen in love with an American soldier. I was a student nurse and I forget who I was enamored of at the time. It was a friendly but superficial occasion and I don't think we referred to the day of our quarrel. She married and went to America a year or two before I did likewise, but after a while we lost touch.

Years went by, and at last, on a trip to Chicago, I managed to rediscover her. I was delighted at the reunion, but again it was one which did not give us the opportunity to really talk. We kept up a correspondence for a short while; but it was at the height of the anti-Vietnam War movement and my life was frantic and chaotic, and once more I lost touch with her: my address book got lost and with it my memory of her married name. As with some other friends, I waited in the hope she would write to me, but she didn't; and as time passed it seemed less and less likely, as their children grew up and left home, that she and her husband would still be living at the same address, even if I could recall it. I did eventually remember her married name as Parker—but how to trace *that* in the huge Chicago area? Who knows—maybe she will read this book, and at least know that I have not forgotten those two years that were the last of our real childhood, and the very best of it.

AN ENCOUNTER
—AND A RE-ENCOUNTER

The boundary between the end of childhood and the beginnings, however rudimentary, of adult life is vague. It resembles border country where two cultures lie side by side, the customs and language of each spilling over into the other for some distance beyond official frontiers; or the marshes of a broad, meandering estuary: what is marsh and what is the many-throated river itself? I did not play one day at Robin Hood or Escaping from Pirates, and the next day join the Young Communist League; these activities, seemingly belonging to different stages of life, overlapped somewhere in that shifting, marshy borderland.

With my sister I often discussed politics. Though she was nine years older she did not take the role of instructor but let me hold forth as if I were an equal. I've no doubt she was in reality highly influential. Nevertheless, when I said to her one day, "You know, Oggie, I've been thinking we ought to join the Communist Party," I was entirely convinced of the independence of my proposal. We were riding home on the upper deck of a bus, late in the afternoon after a long walk somewhere near Chigwell Row. Olga replied that she thought I was probably right: the time had come to take that step.

So the next day we went down to Seven Kings to the Party branch office. At least, the way I remember it we went together; but Stan Robertson, who was at the enquiry desk, says I came alone and that it was Goodmayes, not Seven Kings. "Past the tall, overgrown lilac tree to the front door of 53 Ashgrove Road you came," he wrote to me in 1989—and the concrete details make me incline to think his recollection is correct. "To Goodmayes with words tumbling over themselves: 'My name is Denise Levertoff, I and my sister Olga, she's 21 and I'm 12, we want to join . . .' That unforgettable gush of words made me reflect at the time that if this were *you* then what was your elder sister like? I was soon to discover!"

(Stan was then around her age, and fell seriously in love with her—but that's another story.)

The way *I* remember it, she and I did go together to the office, but I did the talking; so maybe, again, my recollection is faulty, for Olga was notably talkative and it seems somewhat unlikely that I'd have been our spokesperson; on the other hand, she might have been deliberately keeping a low profile to further my sense of autonomous decision. At all events, what stands out to me with absolute clarity is how nonplussed I was when told I was too young to join the party. "But can't I join the Young Communist League?" I enquired, aggrieved. "You have to be sixteen," was the answer. But Stan evidently perceived my disappointment and indignation, for he immediately made a conciliatory suggestion: "You could come and sell the paper on Saturdays, though—?" At which I cheered up. Yes! I had instantly acquired a sort of special membership, even if it didn't come with a card.

So it was that every Saturday morning I would go not to the park or the Borough Library but to meet Stan and another young man or two near the train station, and each carrying an armful of *Daily Workers* we'd go by tram down Ilford Lane towards Barking, where each of us took one side of a street of small working-class houses to canvass. We'd reconvene at each cross-street to compare notes, then take on a fresh block.

Going from house to house I'd knock or ring the bell, and when someone came to the door I'd start my *schpiel*. Often as not, the door would be slammed in my face, but some people listened politely and a few even accepted the paper. (I'm not sure now if it was a free introductory copy or if we collected their pennies.) My speech usually opened with, "Read *The Daily Worker*, the worker's own paper, written *by* workers *for* workers—" I seldom had a chance to say much more.

What always strikes me as extraordinary is that no one ever challenged me as to what *I* was doing delivering this message. At twelve I was fairly tall for my age, but still clearly a child, in knee socks and a reefer coat, with two long braids. I didn't even look or sound like the child of a "worker." Yet no one showed the least surprise or curiosity.

I seem to have found the task of canvassing fairly easy, though later on in my life, when I was involved in anti-war and anti-nuclear organizing activities, I would do anything to avoid having to actually talk to strangers about the issues. I'd stuff envelopes, hand out leaflets,

stick posters on walls, commit acts of civil disobedience,
and even, if obliged to, read poems or make speeches
over faulty P.A. systems to peripatetic crowds at rallies;
but I dreaded the one-to-one talking I seem to have
managed quite blithely as a twelve-year-old Communist.

To me, I suppose, the enterprise had about it some-
thing of the pretend adventures I was leaving behind
me, and yet gave the sober thrill of feeling I was acting
in the real, grown-up world, doing something for the
ideals of righteousness I cherished—a jumble of notions
derived partly from my family's values but also from *Le
Morte d'Arthur, Little Women,* my hero-worship of
Father Conrad Noel (the "Red Parson" of Thaxted,
with his William Morris-style Christian Socialism). And
I knew, of course, about the horrors of Nazism and
Fascism: my parents were already heavily involved in
German refugee aid; Mussolini had invaded Abyssinia;
the Spanish Civil War was raging. To me there was
nothing inappropriate about the way I was spending
those Saturday mornings (though I can't remember dis-
cussing them even with Olga, and something tacitly
warned me that my parents might not approve, liberal
though they were; since no one asked, I had no need to
say where I'd been).

But though it mattered to me at the time—the
adventure of taking on a responsible task along with
people twice my age—the whole experience of making a
"pitch" in those drab streets (for a newspaper I don't
believe it occurred to me to read, but which I regarded
as a symbol of Truth and Justice) might have faded into

the mists of those temporal marshlands if it were not for one memorable incident.

One cold winter day—we'd be blowing on our fingers, warming up with a cup of hot sweet tea from a curbside stand on Ilford Lane when our stint was over—I had rung the bell of a house with particularly shabby curtains in its front-room window and after a few moments was about to turn away, thinking there was no one home, when I heard slow footsteps within. I waited while someone shuffled to the door and opened it. It was a very pale sad-faced man; he didn't look old, exactly, but somehow ghostly, I thought. It was in fact the face of discouragement, of one who once had hope and has none left. A thin, bony-looking man with wispy colorless hair. I had started my sales talk the moment the door began to open—"I want to introduce you to *The Daily Worker,* the only paper written *by* workers, *for* workers," and he just stood there in a collarless shirt, baggy trousers, old felt slippers—just stood and looked at me with pale, sad eyes. He didn't interrupt, but when I came to a halt he said, in a slow, quiet voice, "I haven't worked for years. I've been unemployed for years and years . . . ."

It took the wind out of my ignorant little sails. Abashed, I mumbled something apologetic and turned away as he softly shut his door. I'd seen long lines of men outside the Labor Exchanges as I rode the buses, and all my life I'd been accustomed to the small brass bands of unemployed WWI ex-servicemen playing on major shopping streets all over London. I knew "Unemployment" was one of the big issues of the day. But this was the first time the meaning of the words in somebody's life came home to me.

Although I didn't consciously formulate it, the idea that perhaps what I was doing was presumptuous did dimly start to occur to me as a result of that encounter. And soon all sorts of changes in my life (and in Olga's, in Stan's too—part of that other story, *her* story, which I don't know enough about to tell) brought my Saturday propaganda efforts to an end. Other preoccupations dominated, and though the ideals which had motivated me remained in place, they rarely asserted themselves until the '60s.

Stan had not become a prominent figure in my twelve-year-old consciousness despite our temporary camaraderie on those expeditions, and over the years I'd completely forgotten that for a short time he and Olga had actually been "engaged." That my father had "given him a gentle lecture" on the responsibilities of married life, clearly intended to discourage him, was something I probably didn't know even then. (Stan, too, was unemployed, and anyway not at all what my parents may have hoped for in an eventual son-in-law.) But in any case, it wasn't long before Olga ran off with a much older man, one who was far less "suitable" than Stan, and there was grief and turmoil at home, and I began to spend more and more time in the wholly apolitical world of ballet school. Stan disappeared from view—forever, I would have assumed if I'd thought about it.

But instead, fifty years later he reappeared, by mail; and not any longer (as in vague memory he had become to me) a sort of stick-figure, supernumerary in a faded episode, but a person, a vivid personality, with a devotion to classical music and an abiding concern for social justice. A *friend* emerged from that distant time with his much clearer vision of what for me was a foggy border country. A friend whom I've now met again, on London visits, and whose long wonderful letters are one of the joys of my present life, far away in Seattle.

JINNY

A busker, who played the violin to London theater queues and owned a monkey who collected the pennies, lived somewhere in Ilford and used to take the train from the Ilford station. When I was twelve I began to travel up to town almost every day for my ballet classes and my music, French, and art lessons. If I spotted the man with the monkey I hurried down the platform to be sure of getting into the same compartment with them. These were the transverse railway carriages of English trains, with about six seats on each side; and the local trains had no corridors, so it was necessary to secure a seat next to the monkey from the beginning—one could not get into the back of the train and make one's way along it as it went. The monkey's name was Jinny; she had a black face and beautiful golden-brown fur. The man's wife knitted her little caps and dresses of scarlet or Irish green wool. Jinny was friendly and quite sedate for a monkey. I loved to sit next to her and hold her hand, which was black and very cold.

Sometimes, queuing for the ballet or a play—sitting on the little canvas stools that were handed out to people waiting for unreserved seats—I'd hear the busker's violin and see him and Jinny settle down to perform and collect. Jinny gravely passed the hat and I felt as proud to know her personally as if she had been one of the great dancers or actors I was queuing to see. I never saw her again after the war began.

MEETING AND
NOT MEETING ARTISTS

I. NOT MEETING M. OZENFANT

When I was thirteen, I saw in some art magazine that
Amedée Ozenfant had opened a studio in London. I
knew of him because a book of his was in the local pub-
lic library and I had often borrowed it and browsed
therein, not reading carefully but obtaining from it that
whiff of romance anything associated with artists had
for me. My idea of the life of art students was based
mainly on those scenes in Kipling's *The Light that
Failed* in which from time to time the great teacher
looks in at the students, their easels, their model, the
stove and its long L of black stovepipe, silently contem-
plates them working away day by day and week by
week, and each time, after a little while, utters the
magic words, *"Continuez, mes enfants, continuez,"* and
departs. There was also Svengali and Little Billee, in
Trilby, poverty made merry by comradeship and
dreams. I decided I must study with Ozenfant (whose
name I pronounced as if it were German).

My parents were concerned only for my welfare,
and needed no special persuasion to make enquiries for

me. But how innocent, how ignorant, we were! In the first place, it did not seem to occur to any of us to write, much less to phone. We simply set out, one day, to approach M. Ozenfant. And besides, though I drew and painted for hours every day, I had no outstanding talent and there was no reason whatsoever why, if I were going to study art, I should not take a class at some school of art that took beginners, and not presumptuously apply to a well-known painter.

It was a warm afternoon when we set out, after the Saturday morning service at St. George's Bloomsbury, for the Gloucester Road, or perhaps it was the Cromwell Road, near which the school was supposed to be. We seemed to have to trudge for miles along dusty streets after we got out of the Underground, a forlorn little trio: my father in his clerical overcoat, too heavy for the day and—my mother claimed—"green with age"; my mother always well dressed, small but (in those days) portly, wearing one of the dashing hats she used to create—scarlet, or dark but with a bold feather in it; and I, almost as tall as my not-very-tall father, in knee-socks, my hair in two long braids. I was nervous, excited; they perhaps were nervous too, and solemn.

At last we arrived at the address I had copied from the paper. It was one of those 1/2 numbers, 17 and 1/2 for example, a mews cottage in what was to us the unknown territory where South Kensington and Earls Court begin to blur into each other. A sign on the house door did indeed confirm that this was the right place; but it looked very small indeed for an art school, said my parents dubiously as we stood in the alleyway waiting for someone to answer our ring of the bell. All was silent, however. A cat was inspecting some dustbins under the shuttered groundfloor windows, which flanked a double door that was flush with the pavement, without a doorstep, and not recessed by a porch—a fact that struck me as exotic, appropriate, and somehow Parisian.

Having walked so far, my father was not about to give up without another try. He gave the bell another hard and prolonged push, then rapped the brass knocker as well. And yes, someone was home. An upstairs window was thrown open, and a pale, sleepy face with a rather tousled head of henna-red hair appeared: a lady with a strong French accent asked with some surprise, but no hostility, what we wanted. When she learned that the bearded clergyman and his wife were seeking art lessons for their young daughter her surprise appeared to increase; and no wonder. Certainly I would have to have been a prodigy for the sophisticated author of *La Peinture Moderne,* the post-Cubist "purist," to have taken me on as a student! At all events, it was clearly not for her to decide; but she informed us that M. Ozenfant was in Paris and would not return for two weeks, and that possibly we would wish to write to him later for an appointment. She was amiably, indeed quite delicately, discouraging.

The interchange—my parents' enquiries as to whether M. Ozenfant would consider so young a pupil, and whether he gave classes or only private lessons, and the lady's replies—took place with the three of us standing in the middle of the mews in a row, gazing dubiously up at her, while she, at the window, clutched a bright wrap about her shoulders and didn't offer to come down. It was clear that she wasn't dressed. When I was older I thought it not unlikely that M. Ozenfant was there all the time, in bed in the room behind her. She was, in any case, far more forbearing than her Toulouse-Lautrecian appearance might have led one to expect; gentle towards a child and two unworldly adults who disturbed her from sleep or love.

I can't remember what was said afterwards. I think we went to Lyons for a cup of tea, and after making our way to Victoria got the 25 bus all the long way home. It seems to me it was by tacit agreement that we didn't write to M. Ozenfant. There was a sense of having ventured into a too unfamiliar world; my parents must have realized that this was not the appropriate way to get drawing lessons for a thirteen year old. And as for me, though I had glimpsed a world in which I believed I would one day be at home, I was relieved rather than disappointed to be deferring my entrance into it.

II. MEETING MISS NOAR

Not long afterwards, it was arranged for me to go for weekly lessons with Miss Eva Noar, a member of various professional artists' societies which belonged to a world unknown to the Ozenfants and their kind and was equally unknowing of them. Miss Noar had studied at the Slade School, and for her, the chief modern artists were all English. Wilson Steer was to her a name to be spoken with a reverence whose tone it is difficult for someone unfamiliar with the peculiar insularity of many English artists in the 1930's to imagine. I cannot clearly remember her own work and have never seen it since those days, but I believe it to have been thoroughly craftsmanlike and authentic in its own way, and she was certainly capable of teaching me a great deal had I not, alas, been lazy and probably impertinent; and I did indeed learn something from her, if only how badly I drew. Miss Noar was in her fifties, wore Oxfords, tweed skirts, and short cotton smocks. Every summer she went to Snowdonia for her productive holidays (landscape was her primary subject), and since my mother's family came from Caernarvon and Llanberis, my parents' meeting with her on my initial visit was quite animated. Thereafter, I went alone to my lessons, but Miss Noar did once come for tea to our house in the Essex sub-urbs. I showed her my room, and she exclaimed at the yellow fog floating through the wide-open sash win-dows, and said I was evidently a "fresh air fiend." (Though that acrid chill was hardly "fresh," and I am amazed, in retrospect, at my mother's permitting me to indulge such a craze, when surely the fog must have seeped through from my room to the rest of the upstairs!)

Miss Noar's flat and studio were in Penywern Road, and if it was not raining we often took easels and camp-stools and proceeded to Kensington Gardens to sketch, near the Round Pond or in the vicinity of Kensington Palace. "Pattern, pattern!" Miss Noar would adjure me—for that word *pattern* was her way of summing up all the essential compositional factors. (She may have meant more by it than mere surface decoration: something closer to Hopkins' term, *inscape,* which became so dear to me later on.) Although she and her dictum lacked for me, at twelve or thirteen, the aura of romance, of Paris and *"Continuez, mes enfants,"* yet she succeeded in making me see more. To see—beyond the individual beauties and graces of flower and leaf and cloud, which my mother had revealed to me when I was still almost a baby; or the lacy patterns of bare twigs against pale sky which I'd noticed for myself a little later; or the not dissimilar delicacy of old wrought iron which I had recently discovered at the V. and A.— the complex interaction of three-dimensional objects in space, and their transmutation into compositions: form and colors on a flat surface. I couldn't *do* it, but I did embark upon a lifetime of seeing it.

Somehow, after I had begun to spend the better part of each day at ballet school, my lessons with Miss Noar gradually became less frequent and eventually ceased, either before the War began or just after—a pity, for eventually I came to perceive that I had far more affinity with visual art than with the dance. But at least I can now at long last recognize that Miss Noar, who must have died long since, gave me something of value, and offered more than I was ready to take. Perhaps some day I'll seek and find one of her watercolors of the Welsh mountains. If I discovered one, I would treasure it, whether or not I found I could admire it.

III.   NOT MEETING KOKOSCHKA

At some point during the War, having obtained a nurs-
ing job in Fitzroy Square in the heart of London, I at
last enrolled in an art class. This was at the London
Polytechnic, and the instructor set us to drawing from
plaster casts of Greek and Roman sculpture, just as he
might have a hundred or two hundred years earlier. It
was not exciting, but I liked it anyway and could see
that the practice was beginning to improve my drawing.
But after a few weeks of classes I fell in love and gave
up my studies in order to spend every free moment with
Stephen. My work schedule at the small hospital where
I was employed had been kindly accommodated to my
art classes, and this abandonment of them involved me
in deception and remorse; but youthful love was
stronger than honor, even though I had to carry my
portfolio to all our assignations, an embarrassing
reminder of my dishonesty.

At last the war ended. I was not seventeen when it
started, and now was twenty-two. I was no longer
obligated to work as a nurse (a "reserved occupation"
which had enabled me to escape conscription into the
women's branches of the armed forces, or in a muni-
tions factory, concerning which alternatives I had scru-
ples of conscience as well as extreme distaste, though I
had not arrived at a consistent commitment to non-vio-
lence). I had broken up with my boyfriend and begun to
work at a series of odd jobs. And now I made one more
attempt to study art, this time again with a master
painter.

While hanging around one of the West End galleries, as I often did, I had announced to the curator or manager, with whom I had struck up an acquaintance, that I would like to pose as a model in exchange for lessons, if she knew of someone who might be interested. I had conceived this idea in a spirit of adventure. Astonishingly, she gave me Kokoschka's Hampstead address—and with her name as a reference I made arrangements for a trial visit. I was to bring a drawing block and some charcoal along with me. On the appointed day I arrived punctually at one of those typical, substantial, grayish brick houses, dating from the 1890's, which line many Hampstead streets. It may have been in one of the roads that run west off Haverstock Hill. I was shown into a front room to wait, along with a supercilious young man who evidently had also just arrived, and whose drawings, glimpsed as he shuffled them, were far more advanced than mine. We sat waiting in silence, as in a dentist's waiting room, until he was summoned and I was left to myself. In the featureless room nothing revealed that a painter lived here. Perhaps a clock was ticking; perhaps a fly was buzzing; certainly my heart was thumping. My tensions grew, and suddenly I was seized not by fear but by shame. At some imperfectly articulated level I faced the fact that, all along, my pursuit of art—visual art, that is—had been half-hearted, not a true compulsion. My true vocation was and had always been, virtually from infancy, poetry. I'd had this realization before, in regard to ballet—but with ballet I'd had the excuse that it was my sister who had coaxed me into it, and I had only continued in ballet school as long as I did in order not to lose face, and lose my friends there, "all in one fell swoop." With visual art it was a different story: *looking* at art was already a true, and proved to be a lasting, passion. But though I did have a genuine impulse to *do* it, too, and perhaps some small talent to be developed, I was sitting in that waiting room at that moment, prepared to waste a serious artist's time if I could persuade him to take me on as model and pupil, *not* out of a burning desire to learn but in search of a world: the old imaginary world of *The Light That Failed* and *Trilby*; a world of thrilling conversations and midnight oil and Bohemian *camaraderie;* of the stimulating company of people dedicated to creative vocations. The world, in short, in search of which I had already set out long before, when I convinced my patient parents to call upon M. Ozenfant. Oh, I didn't, certainly, spell it all out to myself in so many words; but I did recognize, in that silent ten minutes (if it was that long—it seemed much longer, as such minutes will) that I was there on false pretences. And in a second I had gathered up my belongings, let myself quietly into the hallway, opened the front door, closed it cautiously behind me, taken the front steps in one bound and was scuttling swiftly up the street and round the corner. I wonder if, finding the room empty, the servant or assistant—a figure of whom I have no recollection—who had admitted me and who must in time have come to fetch me to Kokoschka's presence, checked to see if anything was missing? Or perhaps guessed that courage had failed me; but could not have guessed the whole truth.

It was not, in chronological time, very long before I did come to know a number of painters who became close and lasting friends, and to know other writers too. But by then I had more fully acknowledged both my own identity as a writer and the fact that I could not be a painter *too*, as my greedy dreams had supposed. What of the romantic comradeship? Eventually I came to perceive that (for me at least) this does indeed exist, but— except on the rarest, most ephemeral occasions—in friendships scattered one by one over many continents, not clustered in one place at one time.

CAFÉ ROYAL

When I worked as an Assistant Nurse in a London hospital I went on many of my free evenings to the Café Royal in Piccadily. I knew of it from books and thought of it as a place which artists and writers, scholars and eccentrics, interesting people of many kinds, frequented; and to a certain extent I was right, though it had no doubt passed the days of its glory even before the war. Built in the 1870's it had been done over in 1928 and the café part of it, distinct from the restaurant (which I never ventured into) shared now, with everything else, some of the drabness of war-time and blackout. Too young to make comparisons, I found it good enough for me, with its big mirrors and marble-topped tables; to my near-sighted gaze it had an exciting glitter, and I could sit there for a couple of hours gazing and dreaming, drinking coffee, puffing away at a cigarette (they were rationed, of course, and one smoked them down to the smallest butt), armed with a book so as not look as if I were waiting for anyone.

Almost always I went there alone, but one time I invited Gisela to meet me there. It made me feel properly adult and sophisticated to do so—quite different from going to the cinema or to a soldier's dance with one of my fellow nurses: *that* was a participation in *their* world; *this* was the one I wanted to think I belonged in because I was a poet and artist. Gisela, though younger than I, and here at the café for the first time, belonged in it already because of her writer parents and their friends, and her childhood spent in France and Italy. (I didn't analyze this, but I would not have arranged to meet Nurse Lee or Nurse Collins here, though when I was with them I was fully immersed in our collective experience. I was in fact living simultaneously in several subcultures during those war years, which were also the years of my late and prolonged adolescence. It wasn't a simple matter of English class stratification; it is true that the ambiance of international intellectuals in which Gisela had grown up was certainly more "upper class" and wealthy than that of most of the nurses I knew, but it was not the "upper class" as such but a non-philistine subdivision of it, full of Jews and artists.)

As if to demonstrate the character of the Café Royal, we were spotted that evening by the art historian John Rothenstein, who knew Gisela's parents. After sitting with us for a while he invited us to come and see some painting or other and took us along to his magnificent apartment nearby. I like to think it was in the fabled Albany (shades of Mr. Salteena!)—and perhaps it was. How annoying not to remember what it was he showed us, or what other works hung on his walls: I was dazzled whatever they were—too much so to carry away any clear recollection of what I'd seen or of anything interesting he probably told us in the half hour or so we were there.

More memorable was an old antique dealer with whom I got into conversation—perhaps on more than one evening. He too used to come to the café of an evening to watch the world within the mirrored walls over a stretched-out coffee. He owned roomsful of treasures, he told me, but who wanted to buy antiques in the middle of a war? They were piled up, waiting, and so far had escaped the bombs. Would I like to see? We went out into that darkness no city-dweller born after that time can imagine (and no Americans even if they are older, unless they were there as G.I.'s). Every window tightly covered with opaque black material; no streetlights; virtually no traffic at night, and what there was, lit by only the dimmest of dim headlights. Outer doors were quickly opened and closed, and often a screen just inside further prevented light from escaping. So one came out of a bright interior into thick blackness and had to stand still a moment until the eyes adjusted. If one didn't, one could instantly bump into some obstacle, as I did once, stepping out of a pub with a few drinks in me—right across a narrow sidewalk to collide full tilt with a lamppost, chipping a front tooth and lucky not to have lost it or been concussed. And in that darkness, my companions were hardly aware anything had happened.

With the old antique dealer I plunged again into that familiar yet always startling blackness and was led by him through the streets, northward, to somewhere in Soho. Everyone carried flashlights (torches, one says in England) but used them as little as possible to save on batteries. At his door he produced his to find the keyhole and we climbed several flights of stairs. Wasn't I scared, going off into the dark with an unknown old man, going up to his flat, no one anywhere knowing where I was if I disappeared forever? That's what someone asked me when I recalled this years later. The answer is, no—I can't remember feeling anything but curiosity, the interest one feels in reading a story, wondering what the next page will hold. Did he really have such a heap of treasure, or would it turn out to be a lot of rubbish? Besides, he was a nice old Jewish man, grandfatherly, and a regular customer at the Café Royal.

When we got up to his flat it was indeed crowded with objects—elaborate lamps, inlaid boxes, old portraits in heavy frames, statuary, swags of velvet, vases, silver dishes and candlesticks. My countless hours at the V. and A. before the war began, mooning enchanted among its priceless bric-a-brac, had not made me connoisseur enough to know if this stuff were "good" or not, but it looked like treasure to me, anyway—and very likely it was, for I found out later that he was quite a famous dealer.

So: I saw it, I marvelled, congratulated him, and commiserated with the fact that while the war lasted, his stock-in-trade might accumulate but could not find buyers. His need to show it, as if to prove to himself its existence, was satisfied, and I returned through the night to my hospital, satisfied also: I was "seeing life."

Maurice de Montfaucon was another matter, though. One night a thin small man with a small moustache and an East End accent came over to my table against the wall (were the benches along that wall upholstered in dark red velvet, or am I imagining it?) and asked politely if he and his friend might join me. He indicated a larger man seated a few tables away. I saw no reason to say no, so the other man approached at his friend's nod and they both sat down with me. The second man, who was broader as well as taller, had a big rather handsome head, well-manicured hands, and expensive-looking clothes even in that time of rationing. He introduced himself as Maurice de Montfaucon and his friend as David Gold. David had been his batman before both of them had been invalided out of the army, and had saved his life—or maybe they'd saved each other's lives. Anyway, as civilians they maintained a fast friendship and met often in the evenings.

Evidently something of the older relationship remained, however, for egalitarian though this sounded, Maurice had sent David to my table as his messenger. He liked my face, was curious about me, wanted to see what book I was reading. David joined in the conversation but it was definitely Maurice who led it. He questioned me about my life: no-school childhood, clergyman father originally from Russia, ballet school, wartime nursing, poetry; and seemed baffled but fascinated.

In the ensuing weeks or months I met the two a number of times, sometimes together, sometimes separately. Once I drove around for a whole evening with David, whose job was to pick up the proceeds from pinball machines in pubs. (Looking back, it occurs to me for the first time that this was surely somewhat dangerous. Blacked-out streets, bags of money. . . . In America surely this job would be done in an armored car, and by daylight. But there wasn't much crime in wartime London.) I'd sit in the parked car, he'd bustle in and be out again in a few minutes. Eventually we had a drink at what he considered the best of the pubs on his route, somewhere east of Islington. After getting out of the army, he told me, he had spent some months in Staffordshire at the Hospital for Functional Nervous Disorders, getting cured from a severe, crippling stutter, which indeed was now scarcely detectable. He referred to Maurice with respect and admiration, which I noted. David himself was low-key, polite and good-humoured, and though I don't recall what on earth we talked about I felt at ease with him, whereas Maurice made me shy and uncertain. Both were, I suppose, in their mid to late thirties, which to an immature twenty-one-year-old seemed, if not old, unimaginably experienced, as if they were not only of a different gender but a different species.

What did Maurice do? He claimed to have something to do with films, but was not a director. Perhaps a producer? He spoke about Elstree and studios; but vaguely, and seemed to have other business interests of some kind. Was his grand name real? And the ancestral castle somewhere in France (if it were still there after the war)? He had certainly been an officer in the British Army but of course that meant nothing in wartime. His speech and courtly manners accorded with his implied aristocracy and yet, naive though I was, seemed to me possibly those of an actor playing a Lord—just a trifle exaggerated. Yet it was precisely his flamboyance that made it fun to meet with him as I did. I was nonplussed and embarrassed at his professions of passionate and sincere love for me; they were certainly more appealing than anything a typically reticent upperclass Englishman would have been likely to articulate (though he claimed to be mainly of English descent and upbringing), but I responded only with disbelief. *Why me?* Ach, he told me with exasperation, no, you are quite right, you are not even particularly pretty—if I wanted sirens, don't you understand I have dozens of lovely starlets to choose from? Why you? But . . .

He didn't succeed in articulating what he saw in me and I continued to conclude he was just teasing, a form of idle flirtation. I didn't know how to flirt back and it was irritating. But I continued to meet him some evenings anyway, because somehow I liked him and was intrigued. Strange as it may seem, I can't remember if he ever kissed me, or tried to. I was not a virgin, only very ignorant and unawakened, and I would not have stopped him, I suppose, though if it had been a sloppy wet kiss I would not have let it happen again. In any case we met only in the Café Royal, and London was not Paris where people kiss in public!

So trusting was I that when he had the flu I took a bottle of cough syrup and some precious oranges (which for the first time in years had miraculously become available, strictly rationed) and went to his flat for the first and only time. I was wearing my nurse's uniform (minus the cap) for I had to go on duty quite soon—our strange schedules meant that I sometimes had three hours off in the middle of the day. I felt a little shy, but not apprehensive.

This lack of fear—going alone to the apartments of strange men, whether an old antique dealer or the ambiguous Maurice (and there were other adventures unconnected with the Café Royal) was less a personal characteristic than an effect of the historical moment. Most people in London were not in a constant quake of terror; of course we felt terror, often enough, during an actual bombing, but in between sirens people went calmly about their business, as is well-known. We were entirely used to the darkness of the blackout. At those periods when it had seemed Hitler might invade—might win—that thought was utterly frightening, of course; yet it was only a thought which came and went—one shuddered, and got on with whatever one was doing. This collective response made it seem, to a person of my age, as if other things about which one might otherwise have had doubts and hesitations were equally to be taken for granted. My Sister of Mercy visit to Maurice was no more alarming in prospect than it proved to be in fact.

His flat was in a smallish building squeezed between two large ones, somewhere just south of Piccadilly, rather posh, with a buzzer system at the door, the first I'd ever encountered. The two flights up to his floor were wide and shallow. The door to his flat was open, as he'd told me it would be, and he called to me from the bedroom, where he sat up in bed backed by a lot of pillows, looking flushed and feverish and coughing quite a lot. He was wearing a blue satin robe over his pyjamas. I sat down on the edge of the bed, felt his fore-head with the back of my hand, gave him the oranges. He started to laugh at my nursely air but it made him cough to laugh so he confined himself to florid expressions of gratitude and undying devotion. I fetched a spoon from his minute kitchen for the cough mixture and insisted that he take some, but I had one eye on my watch, and it was very soon time to go or I'd be late on duty. On the way out I glanced around the living room and saw that a large oblong table was entirely covered with identical large cardboard boxes the way the old dealer's was with antique objects; I had the impression he was selling something, as well as whatever it was he did in the film industry.

By the next time I saw him I'd met one of the loves of my life, a young man only a few years older than I; this was serious emotional business and since I didn't take Maurice seriously but did regard him as a friend of sorts, I told him about it. He was furious; at least, he tried to make me believe he was, but wasn't he overacting? Little fool, he shouted, gripping the table and making the coffee cups shake in their saucers, you want some idiotic boy when you have a real man who's crazy about you!

I didn't see him for months after that, for I stopped going to the Café Royal and spent all my free time with my boyfriend, if he was free too, or brooding about him when he was not. Maurice was not in my thoughts at all.

But I did encounter him one more time. Every third week I had three days off at a time, and I was on my way to Charing Cross to catch a train. My closest friend at that time was somewhat alienated by my preoccupation with this young man, and as I was not so besotted with love as to take a breach of friendship calmly, I was rushing down to the south coast to find her before she moved (for she was about to change jobs).

The escalators in the Tottenham Court Road tube station are long ones; and civilized etiquette in England is that people stand on one side only, leaving a clear passage for those in a hurry (unlike the U.S., where people clog the entire width of the steps). As I ran down, I caught sight of Maurice ascending. He gave a tremendous start when he saw me, swung round, and began frenziedly running down the up escalator.

And that's when I did feel fear. I'd never known what to make of him, how to place him in any way; but there was no need to as long as he remained an insubstantial figure at the edge of my life. He'd never been anywhere near center stage, as close friends were, such as the one I was hoping to see in Sussex, or as my boyfriend was. But now the intensity with which he was crazily bucking the escalator's imperturbable tide to try and catch me seemed to break out of the insubstantial: he was incomprehensible but suddenly real, authentic. Did this older man, then, really love me, as he claimed? Who was he, what was he? He'd not made the usual passes or pestered me to see him oftener, or to come to his flat. (That one visit when he had the flu had been my own idea.) He was such a mystery to me that I'd not been able to describe him to my friends, to get an independent view of him.

Confronted now by a force to which I had no idea how to react, I panicked. That force was so much larger than I was, and spoke a language I didn't know—and surely was incapable, in turn, of understanding mine. I could handle straddling a couple of subcultures, but I couldn't deal with a man whose realities of life, values, pursuits, beliefs and emotions were unfathomable to me and yet who demanded a response. Even more disturbing was the apprehension that he had no more clue to me than I to him—what he perceived, whatever it was, was not my *me*.

Air-raids, the blind, blacked-out streets? Routine. Old men whose midnight attics could have been filled with Bluebeard horrors, not respectable antiques gleaming by torch-light? Nonsense! But Maurice de Montfaucon tearing down the up escalator—! Fear!

I reached the bottom before him, ran down the corridor, round a corner, and into a train just as the doors shut. I never saw him or David Gold again, and he never enquired for me by phone or letter. And I still wonder.

ORACLES

Twice, in my youth, an oracle prophesied that I would have an extraordinary life. At seventy, it seems to me that they were right, though neither of them foresaw the manner of it.

The first time, when I was seven, the oracle was a clever young designer of hats, whose little boutique, where in the back room his wife helped his creations to materialize, was frequented by my mother and teen-aged sister in the millinery-conscious early thirties. On this occasion my sister was not present, but was the subject of conversation; attractive and variously gifted, people were always asking about her and complimenting my mother on her daughter's achievements. At this time she was practicing for her LRAM—the piano diploma that few people ventured to try for at sixteen, as she did. For hours a day our house rang with Liszt and Chopin, Albeniz and Bach. (She passed in Performance but failed in Theory, and refused to sit the exam again the following year.)

While my mother tried on hats and discussed Olga with the hatshop man, I was quietly trying on hats myself. There were so many different ones, so many different shapes, textures, colors! Hats with flowers, hats with feathers; turbans, brims. . . . I would put them on my head, carefully, one after another, making a grown-up face at myself in the mirror. I knew exactly which I liked—and quickly put aside with a grimace those I didn't approve of.

It was absorbing, and I was not really listening to the talk going on behind me though I was vaguely aware of its familiar theme. But suddenly I distinctly heard him say, in a changed tone, "But *this* one"—and then something like—"she's really going to be something special!" Those exact words sound too American and too contemporary; but they convey the gist of what actually followed those first three: "But *this* one!" After that he went on to make some further comment like, "Because she knows exactly which she likes," or, "what she likes."

I was astonished (after all, all I was doing was playing with the hats!) and I think it is true that I was awestruck. I already had become aware of feeling within me, not yet articulated, that I would in time encounter wonders, do . . . what, I could not formulate, but something which would ensure that my life would not be dull and drab. No doubt it was already clear to me that my parents and sister were not dull and drab, so that this feeling about myself was in some degree merely a reasonable expectation. Nevertheless there was something awesome, portentous, and *confirming* about hearing someone who scarcely knew me single me out in this way. What was "special" about knowing which hats I liked and didn't like?

It must have been his change of tone, from the ordinarily chatty to a moment of revelation, that I picked up, more than the words themselves. I didn't let on that

I'd heard—how embarrassing *that* would have been! And soon we left, my mother pleased with her new hat. She made no reference to his remark, and of course I didn't either. Did she guess that I'd overheard, or not?

What is strange is that in all the years, I never asked her about the incident. But it had flooded me with lasting feeling.

In the seventies my friend Jon and I would talk about the sense of *having a destiny,* which both of us had had from an early age. It's a kind of extension of the sense of identity, of being an *I,* a *me.* When a sense of destiny is added to that awareness, it says to one not, "You are more important than anyone else," or "You are the true center of the world".—nothing like that—but: "You will not have a dull existence, life's events will have significance for you." In a child's terms, it would be more like, "You will have exciting adventures—interesting things will happen to you," or even, "Your life will be a story." But of course a child of seven does not verbalize it; these are only retrospective attempts at doing so. A couple of years later, though, the feeling did crystallize into almost words, in the form of an unspoken awareness that I was some kind of artist person, although at that time painting was as important an expectation as writing, and for a time I hoped to be a dancer as well.

The second oracle spoke about thirteen years later. My friend Marya and I, answering an ad, went to be interviewed for nursing jobs in Ealing (one of London's inner suburbs). The place turned out to be a large private house on a dreary street (the kind from which the cliché, "It had seen better days," is inseparable). It was now a nursing-home full of senile bedridden residents; the rooms were overcrowded with iron bedsteads, dirty linen was heaped on the floor outside bedroom doors instead of in decent wheeled baskets, the place smelled of urine and we knew at once (exchanging a secret look) that we'd die rather than work here. However, we were young and always hungry, and in those days of rationing one did not refuse a hand-out; so we accepted an invitation to have tea with the staff. (We were clearly being wooed; they must have been constantly losing employees and trying to hire new ones.)

Tea was served in the big Edwardian dining room at a large table, with Matron sitting at the head of it with a big teapot. There was plenty of cake and bread-and-butter; and it was quite an entertaining experience, too, because Matron had a guest who offered to read everyone's tea cups.

The usual dark handsome men and long voyages, the giggles and teasing, ensued as the tea-leaf reading took place, and though Marya and I despised the place in our judgmental and superior way (and it really was a miserable, substandard establishment, though perhaps not actually a place of abuse and intentional neglect), we were not above joining in with mild enjoyment. But then came my turn and the oracle spoke.

It was really quite strange. Just as a gypsy lady had once suddenly stopped her ordinary patter and begun to speak to my mother in a wholly different, tranced manner, prophesying—and not gladly—future troubles for my sister, so this woman, about whose appearance I remember nothing and who had seemed till then absolutely unremarkable, startled not only me but the whole company (four or five nurses, Matron, Marya) as she began to speak rapidly and in a different voice. She seemed to see something big, something impressive, a future for me that was altogether astonishing and which she hardly knew how to utter.

No doubt because of the context, my being here to apply for an Assistant Nurse's position, she interpreted her intuition in medical terms. "You have healing powers—healing—great powers—you will be a great healer," she stammered. Everyone was poised, listening to her—no one was passing the cake or giggling: a tense moment that seemed endless. I can't remember how it broke and ordinary talk resumed, or how we made our adieux and departed. And though Marya and I were close friends we didn't really speak of it, dismissing it with an embarrassed laugh, for we knew I was not dedicated to nursing nor very good at it and would quit as soon as the war ended.

Yet on a deeper level I was aware that something had seized the woman in the midst of a parlor game: she'd perceived *something* that must be real. Could it be that I *ought* to stay in nursing, or explore some related medical field? It didn't seem in the least appropriate, and yet—?

But in time I came to feel she had spoken in those terms only because of the circumstances, and that, like the hat-shop man, she had glimpsed something true about me: that I did have *something* to give, something larger than myself—something which at all events would ensure me an interesting life.

THE VOICE

Some truck—a lorry to us hitch-hiking English girls—
deposited us in Montélimar, nougat capital of the
world. Everything was still in short supply, the summer
of '47, but somehow there managed to be nougat in
Montélimar. We had very little money to spend, but this
was worth a sacrifice. We bought some of the lovely
white, sticky, nut-speckled stuff immediately and
strolled down the street munching it. Bet and I had been
on the move since early morning, walking or hitching
rides along dusty country roads, talking to each other
or, when we succeeded in getting a ride, to our drivers,
whose idiomatic French, or perhaps dialects, we didn't
always understand. Most of our rides had brought us to
small crossroads or the entrances to avenues leading to
farms, until now when we found ourselves in the heat
of the day amid the small town's minor bustle.

Seeking shade and a place to sit down with our
nougat—a luxury of sweetness remembered from pre-
war childhood—we sauntered along the street and,
coming to a church, turned aside to enter it without one
of us even having to say to the other, "Shall we take a
look?" If one has grown up walking in the country in
England, it is of course that one takes a look inside

every village church, for its architecture, its monuments and a few moments of cool stillness.

The heavy doors closed behind us; it was dark, and cool indeed after the hot bright sunlight. We slipped off our rucksacks quietly and found a place to sit. A priest was almost inaudibly murmuring at the altar, and two old women in black were hastily giving the responses, like children saying the multiplication tables. Bet and I were glad to sit quietly and experience this otherness after all the hum and glare—this other rhythm slowly pulsing counter to the quick beat of the world outside these thick stone walls. But now something unexpected: behind a grille to the right of the sanctuary, women's voices began to sing. A choir—a hidden choir. I guessed that they were nuns; and so completely hidden from view were they that I also guessed they were of an enclosed order. I whispered that to Bet. No one would ever see them.

They sang *a capella:* what, I have no idea; but one voice began to mount like a skylark and detach itself from the rest, from those mingled voices which together sounded well, but from whose conjunction this single one soared in an intensity of beauty—a voice so clear and just, yet vibrant with such warm sweetness, I have remembered it always. Or have remembered at least what words and images might have described it: the pure, silvery, cold quality of a coloratura conjoined with something dark, honeyed, sensuous, such as one expects to find only in mezzo-sopranos and contraltos.

To Bet and me, beginning to shiver in the sunless cavern, the fact that this great, this glorious and rare voice was singing behind bars, that the face and identity of the singer would be forever unknown to us and to the world, shadowed the music and gave us a morbid thrill. We did not consider "the greater glory of God," or the fact that the nun may have been perfectly content in her chosen cloister. Yet we were not so young nor so vulgar as to imagine her a prisoner. Mainly, I believe, we were awed to think this treasure was so hidden.

I remember nothing else about our day in Montélimar.

More than three decades later I heard that voice again in a dream. But then it was a boy's voice, my son's, singing soprano as he never had actually sung; my son as a boy of thirteen, his song soaring above a choir and floating outwards, towards me, from some darker, narrower space where he and others were gathered. His music floated free and moved like smoke through the upper air, over the heads of other listeners, to where I stood near the entrance of the great hall. I could no more see him than I could see the nun behind the convent grille at Montélimar, but I knew it was he, his song reaching me, and I rejoiced.

PILGRIMAGE

In the hot Provençal afternoon only I and the cicadas
are awake. Back at our cottage, husband and baby are
asleep, and as I passed through the village all the shut-
ters were closed; cats and dogs dozed in the doorway
shadows. I have forgone the siesta in order to arrive at
the house on the Chemin des Lauves that was Cézanne's
studio at the hour when it supposed to open. I coast
down hills, skim along the flat, trudge up the trafficless
roads on foot, pushing my ancient bicycle. The air quiv-
ers, blue and green. I am a human ant, moving across
this painted landscape over which le Mont Ste. Victoire
presides—aloof judge, ever-changing unchangeable
belovéd, massive geometry of rock.

When I come to the house, a small villa to the left of
the road, the shutters are still closed and there's no sign
of life. Shall I be disappointed? Will it turn out to be
closed after all? I push my bike across the gravel, lean it
against the house wall, and approach the door at the
side of the house which appears to be the one in use. I
press the bell. Nothing happens. I wait, calming
myself—I'm a bit out of breath and feeling the simmer-
ing heat. I press it again, more firmly.

This time there are sounds within. I hear shuffling

footsteps slowly approach. A guard-chain is unhooked, and the door opens a crack to reveal a thin old woman, bare-armed in a cotton chemise—the caretaker, whom I had roused from her siesta, and who seems surprised and somewhat alarmed. When she takes in that it's just a young English woman who wants to see the studio she is reassured, and asks me to wait a moment. She leaves the door ajar and I can hear her within, pouring water into a basin, shuffling about, opening and closing a drawer. After a while she returns, her thin wisps of hair still wet. She has splashed the sleep from her face with cool water and put her faded cotton dress on, but is still wearing slippers. "Come," she tells me.

She leads me up a flight of stairs and throws open a door to a large room. "Voilà!" This had been Cézanne's studio. Promising to bring me a glass of water, she leaves me there unattended after half-opening the shutters so that a tempered light illumines all that is there. I stand speechless in the middle of the room.

Is this really 1951? Did Cézanne really die in 1906, or has he just been gone from here a few weeks, long enough for the pale dust of a hot dry countryside to sift in and coat the familiar objects I see disposed here and there—the black clock, the china statuette of a putto, certain vases and pots, the folds of a woven table-cover against which he would set apples as villages are set against the buttress folds of a mountain? On the day-bed there's a rumpled carriage-blanket—surely he left it so when, unable to rest, haunted always by the implacable demands of the current *motif*, he got up from a brief siesta and seized his hat and his painting gear again and went out into the blazing afternoon, just days ago? Might he not return at any time? Am I not intruding?

Everything in the room has this air of use, of being only recently in use, abruptly (but only temporarily) abandoned as if for a journey taken on impulse.

I walk round the studio on tiptoe, looking at each object or piece of furniture but not touching. The care-taker after a long time returns with a glass. I thank her, and as I drink the water she chatters to me a little; I apologize for disturbing her, she politely demurs, asks where I had come from, how long I've been in France— we're just making conversation. I'm too full of the extraordinary sense of having entered something of Cézanne's life, not a museum, not a relic, to be aware of what we are saying.

At length I perceive it is time to go. I'm too young, naive, and poor to even think about offering a tip. (Only years later I wonder if I should have, or would that have been insulting?) I thank her, she leads me down the stairs; *au revoir, milles mercis, Madame.* I hop on my bike and away.

What was the history of Cézanne's studio between 1906 and 1951? I have no idea. The fact that it was a museum open to the public was known at the time I went there, but no one I met in those months when I lived a few kilometers from it had seen it, and it was evident that the old caretaker (who one could almost have believed to date from Cézanne's own day) was rarely called upon to show the studio to anyone. Everything in it was so unguarded, so simply *there,* where it had the simple right of things-in-use to be, a community of *nature morte* models in waiting. How easily it could have been despoiled by souvenir hunters! But no, it was an island broken off, as it were, from the continent of Time.

I never went back, and my husband never went to corroborate what I had experienced. We moved to Italy soon after.

And I'm sure that now the studio on what Cézanne knew as Chemin des Lauves (renamed the Ave. Paul Cézanne) must be efficiently managed, the dust long removed, the objects labelled, little ropes arranged to keep one from getting too close to anything, a guardian always keeping his eye on visitors. Aix, I'm told, has changed like other places, and probably has grown out to incorporate that isolated country road.

My dream-like half-hour, breathing the very air the grand, grim, passionate old hero humbly and doggedly breathed, remains in me as one of my intangible, inviolable treasures. There was a palette there, brushes, tubes of paint, easels, a lay-figure; his old cloak hung on a peg. The mind, the eyes and hands of Cézanne, the intensity of his sensations, passed into his work; but left some residue in that place. Here, as well as in the open air (where he returned again and again to his chosen sites) he engaged in forging, as he declared he would, his "own blue link" in the chain of artists' vision "from the reindeer on the walls of caves to the cliffs of Monet." The thought of it vibrates in me as it did when I first took Gerstle Mack's *Paul Cézanne* out of the Ilford Public Library when I was 13, already in love with the lilt of pineboughs over *Le Lac d'Annecy* in the

National Gallery. The vision of art, the act of making paintings or poems, a life of doing that. It vibrates with the shimmer of heat he often could hardly bear but in which he went on working; it vibrates with the tingling sound of cicadas, awake when all else is sleeping.

A LOSS

The leather luggage strap I used around my suitcase when I travelled in the sixties and seventies—that strap had a history: In 1913 my mother had been to see her relatives in Wales after the death of her first-born, Philippa. On her way to rejoin my father in Leipzig, when she was about to go aboard the North Sea ferry at Hull, her suitcase was damaged by careless porters, and a seaman, witnessing her distress, gave her this sturdy strap, which served her and then me for so many years. Now it has disappeared—perhaps lent to my son and lost, or perhaps resting in some corner of my attic. I search for it without success.

Its loss nags at me: no one but I knows and feels its true worth, though it is still a useful object, wherever it may be. Only I see it going with my parents and sister Olga from Germany to Denmark in 1919 when they were Displaced Persons, though the term did not yet exist. Only I see it going from Southampton to New York when my mother ventured into the New World at 70, and two years later to Mexico where she was to remain for two decades until her death. She gave it to me one time when I was visiting her there, saying truly that her travels were over. It held my often overfilled and battered cases together as I flew all over the U.S., and back and forth to Oaxaca to see her, and to Europe; it came to Moscow with me in 1971, and to Hanoi in 1972. Now I feel something more than my suitcase is insecure without it—but probably I must live the rest of my life without finding it again. Treasure by treasure falls away.

LOST BOOKS

How much of what I feel impelled to write (in prose, though not in poetry) has to do with loss! It's the universal impulse, I suppose, to set up memorials, to incise upon urns the praise of those whose ashes they hold, on gravestones the dates of birth and death, epitaphs upon stone tablets, lambs and seraphs carved in marble or limestone, ancient graffiti scratched into the walls of ruins.

Lost books haunt me, for these, though lost, are not dead nor utterly irretrievable. Book dealers and libraries have not so far been able to find me a copy of *The Griffin,* but I still hope to reread it before I die—a wonderful children's book published in England in the late '20s or early '30s. I don't know the author's name, but the story is about three children, Ralph, Fulke, and Lal, who go to stay at their mother's ancestral castle while she recovers her health in the South of France. Their uncle Jocelyn is as poor as they and their mother are, and the castle, to his and their despair, may have to be sold if it is not to fall into complete decay. But with the help of a heraldic griffin who comes to life, the children manage to discover, after foiling the plots of a sinister amphisbaena, the secret of where the long-lost family treasure is hidden. I lent the book—a treasure to *me*—to someone in New York City in the 1960's, I believe. Surely there's reasonable hope of finding a copy somewhere. . . .

But *Heylyn's Cosmography* I can never hope to own again; though I know I can at least look at a copy in the rare book library at Stanford. It was the circumstances of my own acquisition of this volume that made it so dear to me, however; and there's no hope that that particular copy could have survived. I was probably ten or eleven when Mr. Bull the mason came to do some repair work on our house, and noticed that I liked books and that my room had some *National Geographic* maps pasted on its walls. He had recently worked on a church belfry somewhere and had found there this tattered and worm-eaten copy of the *Cosmography;* he decided to give it to me. It was missing most of its binding, but by way of compensation for its bad condition, someone in the 18th century had inserted among its loose pages a number of extra prints of ships and places, and some extra maps. The text itself seemed pretty complete, and its 17th-century title page was intact—1665. Peter Heylyn lived from 1599 to 1662, and the title page said, "Cosmography in four books. Containing the chorography and history of the whole world, and all the principal kingdoms, provinces, seas and isles thereof. By Peter Heylyn. With an accurate and approved index . . . Revised, corrected, and enlarged by the author himself immediately before his death . . . London, printed for P. Chetwind, 1665."

What especially delighted me in Mr. Bull's gift was

that he had found it in a belfry. Who had left it there? And when? Might a boy (or even a girl!) enamored, as I was, of ships and maps, the idea of voyages to far places, places mysterious and full of brilliant colors, amazing birds, flowers, trees, and people—could such a child have sought refuge from lessons and chores and taken the big volume secretly up the winding stairs to that church tower, to hide out there and read in peace among the silent weekday bells? And then, in the *Cosmography* itself were included not only maps and accounts of islands and continents so far as they were known in Heylyn's time, but also of lands of fable and fiction: More's *Utopia,* and other imagined countries and diverse societies. Even on the modern map of the South Pacific, pasted on my bedroom wall, there were minute but named isles and atolls marked "existence doubtful," which gave one the delicious illusion that it was still possible to sail off on voyages of geographical discovery—a pleasure no child has today, I suppose. But the charts and engravings in my Heylyn were more concrete and descriptive. All the tales with which Othello courted Desdemona were to be found in those foxed, worm-holed pages, their soft paper crumbling dustily under my hands.

The *Cosmography* came with me to the New World when I married, packed in the old trunk my father had used as a young man in his travels in the Russian and Austro-Hungarian Empires and to what was then known as the Levant. It moved with me to three different New York City apartments, in the course of time, and then to three different addresses in and around

Boston. Somehow, though—carelessly wrapped in brown paper as it was—someone, on its last move, must have thought it was rubbish and thrown it out. I searched and searched; and even when I moved to the Northwest in 1989, still hoped it would turn up as I packed for the movers. But no. My own belfry-discovered gift from Mr. Bull is gone forever, and I can only visit the better-preserved but, to me, impersonal copies to be found in Rare Book collections. . . .

SOME HOURS IN THE LATE '70s

Today's my last in Tonga. By afternoon I should be air-borne for Pago-Pago—two days there, more or less, then to L.A., to friends and news-from-home. At dawn a fierce rain thrummed on the tin roof of my *fale*. The green serpentine coil of pyrethrum incense from Hong Kong burned its eight hours and then the mosquitoes resumed their gourmet meal. Nothing like a light, female, European skin. A rooster crowed a few times close to the hut's back wall (made of woven branches). I got up and stumbled in my thin nightgown over the grass and miniature burdocks to the toilets—no one to see me this early. The rain was only a drizzle by then, the sky an undecided clutter of cloud and pale streaks of an approximate turquoise. I returned to bed to try and catch another hour of sleep, after smearing my newest bites with a quaintly labelled but quite effective anti-itch ointment still manufactured somewhere in New Zealand but once, probably, familiar enough in England. I lay there for a time half-awake—then I must have slept, for a dream intervened: my father's classically disordered study, dismantled after his death twenty-five years ago, has been refurbished. It is still dominated—or rather presided over—by the beautiful but slightly wrong-in-scale, not quite life-size, marble statue of Jesus the Teacher, which used to cause passersby to stop and stare from across the street, for it was visible in the uncurtained upstairs window, pale, human, not at all what anyone expected to see in Ilford, Essex. In the dream, the dust and the heaped papers it was unthinkable to disturb were gone, and in their place were the small easy chair, upholstered in yellow corduroy, and the russet sofa, that furnish my living room in Massachusetts—along with pleasant rugs, lots of space, and of course, tables and desks for Father's ancient vari-type machine and his other necessities; all organized attractively, without rigidity but without the discouraging jumble of old enterprises uncompleted. My father, aged maybe sixty-five?—no older—is pleased, he looks buoyant and fresh. A good dream. Oh, rosy face and bright eyes, I wish I knew you, had known you better; that I knew with suprarational certainty that there was some dimension out of time and space, where I *would* at last know you. I remember your kind, smooth, strong hands, short-fingered (unlike the exquisite long fingers of the stone Jesus), warm and (like my mother's) pleasantly dry. . . .

Tongan voices are shouting and calling; it is quite possible my watch stopped for a while in the night, as it does if I take a sleeping pill and lie very still; it starts again when I move. Time to rise, anyway. I dress, fit the last bits and pieces into my two suitcases and the shoulder-bag. At the washing place by the toilets I look in the one mirror (hung on the men's side, for shaving) and note my sunburned face while I drag a comb through hair frizzy from sun and sea water on top of an old perm. Then I cross the stretch of sand, from which coconut palms, impatiens, and frangipani sprout insouciantly, handsome hens of indeterminate breed scratching among them with their troupe of fostered ducks or what, as a child, I used to make grown-ups laugh by calling, "girls of fifteen or so," the half-grown pullets. When I get to the restaurant, there's André the owner, a solid, humorous Parisian said to be ridden somewhat by the extensive family of his Tongan wife, Alissi, but cheerful withal and seemingly as much in control as he wants to be. And with him there's Jean-Marie, his twenty-two-year-old chef (not that André is not himself a chef, but it's Jean-Marie, a graduate of the exacting French state schools of cookery, who does most of the daily work). They are on the terrace looking out at the stormy sea. Rain is beginning again, a squall which caught me just as I stepped over the frangipani roots on my way in. "Look, look, Denise, dolphins!" André tells me—and I put my glasses on in a hurry and see the rise and fall of dark round heads just beyond the reef. But they are teasing me, and are quick to kindly say so. Not dolphins, divers. Some crazy fishermen out in the coral. Yesterday, though, Jean-Marie and I really did see a dolphin—just one; separated from its friends, or maybe we just missed seeing the others. It gave an unmistakable jubilant leap.

The coral is poisonous. I don't understand why saltwater wounds suppurate, but they do. Last night Peter, the eighteen-year-old Australian, who got bashed against the coral yesterday morning, was telling me he

might have to see a doctor. I'd seen André carefully min-
istering to him, like an old soldier (which I suppose he
is—no older than I but of a harsher grain, scraped by
his life and temperament; yet tempered, too, gentled
into a stoic good humour I may never attain). He was
bathing Peter's wounded arm and foot in barely cooled
boiled water, and applying an ointment of some sort. It
was while Peter was telling me he wasn't getting much
relief from this treatment that he also told me that his
mate, or buddy (who was here already when I arrived,
Peter joining him a week later), was sick with a venereal
disease. It could be gonorrhoea but they're afraid it's
syphilis.[*] Peter thought Ray had already spoken of this
to me, but if he did I hadn't understood him, what with
his thick Sydney accent and the fact that he's been
drinking day and night. When I arrived here almost a
month ago, Ray seemed interested only in swimming
and sunbathing—amazingly capable of lying for hours
on the beach in blazing heat. He did at least swathe his
head in a towel topped by a straw hat. For two days,
since he seemed to eat at early hours and retire to bed at
dusk, rising at dawn to swim again, we scarcely met
except to say hello in passing. Then he came and sat by
me on the sand one day and talked a bit. He seemed a
nice, ignorant, innocent nineteen-year-old whose yellow
curls, snub nose, and sun-raw complexion appeared, in
their immaturity, of a piece with his opinions and
desires: he had not wanted to go further in school nor
to tie himself to a job of any kind, but simply to see the

[*] N.B. This was before the AIDS epidemic.

world—not the world of great cities, of Europe and America and Asia, but that of isles and atolls, sandbars and reefs, the Pacific and its rolling surf. It did not occur to him to wonder about the thoughts of the indolent, amiable people of these islands, whose frequent laughter does not strike me as mocking but rather as being without reference to anything non-islanders might construe as amusing. But this incurious Ray, seemingly content with a vegetative existence, has taken to drinking more and more since Peter arrived, and they go off to town every day and often in the evening. He spends less time in the water and on the beach; and he's taken to wearing the brightly flowered kilt or sarong men wear in the South Pacific. He seems to go in for gold, orange, bright yellow in his shirts, too, which match his hair but intensify the unpleasing red of his scorched face.

Peter is a calmer, brawnier, steadier youth, though even younger than Ray, and I haven't attributed Ray's drinking to his influence; indeed, last night he told me it worried him. And then he told me this morning about the V.D. It seems clear Ray has been getting stewed from sheer panic. He knows he's sick and has done absolutely nothing about it. Yesterday he did make some comment to me, in trying to describe the Nukualofa nightlife I've not seen, about what he disgustingly calls the "fucka-girls"; but I thought he was only referring to their existence and their unmistakable appearance. (Judging by the only ones I've seen, they are distinguished only by their outstanding beauty; but that may not be true of all of them. The two I saw came to the restaurant one night with a couple of commercial-traveler types from Australia. The girls were slender, alert, and delicate-looking, unlike the majority of women I've seen here, who quickly grow fat once out of childhood and whose faces lack vivacity. I felt sad that these fascinating, ravishing creatures felt compelled to consort with such coarse escorts. Probably Ray had not been able to afford anything comparable.)

When Peter began telling me Ray was sick, and scared of seeing a doctor, I realized that Ray, last night, may have been trying to tell me so himself, get some advice, and I'd failed to understand. Now Peter, not by agreement but because he himself is scared, has become an intermediary. I told Peter he should go in to see a doctor about his infected foot, even if it's feeling better, just to get Ray to go along. Once they're at the hospital it should be easier to get Ray seen to—Peter could tell the doctors if Ray himself hung back. Ray could get deported from Tonga, it seems, for not reporting his condition—and apparently he would be sent, not back to his (no doubt appalled, but one hopes concerned) parents in Australia, but, because of Australia's stringent laws, which make citizenship a constant probation, to England, where he was born in a village in County Durham and whence he was taken "down under" at age two. There, presumably full of penicillin but totally unfitted for cold weather, jobless and surfless, his already alarming alcoholic tendencies would probably push him further downhill. I suppose it was unacknowledged loneliness, before Peter showed up, that—with innocent curiosity and sheer crass ignorance—got Ray into the town's cheapest brothel, and probably with a woman everyone knew was infected, but, with blurry detachment, failed to warn him about. It's a version of live and let live: live and let die. Of course, who'd have supposed that he'd be too scared to seek treatment! And then there's the question of money, no doubt. He doesn't know what a cure will cost him. Living in these flimsy cabins and eating at André's restaurant is a great bargain, but he's been here many weeks already; and how long can the five hundred dollars he told me he'd saved from a gas-station attendant's job somewhere on the New South Wales coast after he dropped out of high school, possibly last?

On Sunday the odious Mrs. Groby had remarked his unquestionably odd appearance and was sneering at him. The Grobys had come out from town for their usual Sunday dinner. (How can they want a hot, heavy, meat meal at blazing tropical midday?) Afterwards they sit on the beach for a while. He bathes, she doesn't. They bring their mat and their peculiarly affectless dog (her one love, it appears, though I suppose she thinks quite well of Duncan, her husband, a quiet chap with pleasant manners who never contradicts her). The dog causes a certain amount of fuss because he refuses to go in the water. A few weeks ago, paddling around happily enough to all appearances, a wave overtook him and he sank like a stone; since when, understandably, each foamy encroachment of the incoming tide strikes him as an attack. He sits well back, head on paws but eyes warily open, and is deaf to pleas and commands. Therefore he is condemned to wear a flea-collar, which for some reason stains the white fur of his neck (he's black-and-white, of vaguely spaniel ancestry) a sickly shade of tangerine.

Mrs. Groby—Elizabeth—had turned her attention to Ray, whom she happens not to have seen on previous Sundays. I say her attention, but that's imprecise: it's the direction, here or there, of her prepared antipathy. Ray, hanging about near the wooden terrace of the restaurant, is not, it's true, a prepossessing sight with his blotchy scarlet face and shoulder-length yellow ringlets; the garish orange and aqua patterns of his Hawaiian shirt and Tongan male sarong; the whole topped by a pork-pie hat. He looks mildly transvestite, and Elizabeth probably supposes he's what she would call "a homo." She doesn't mind that in Jacques, however, who likes *her,* and, his English being very limited, imagines she likes *him.* She tolerates Jacques because he is discreet (in her presence) and dresses without flamboyance. Behind his back she is not complimentary, and is certainly not going to help him out of his scrape, as he fancies—but that's another matter. Meanwhile she has found in Ray an object ready-made for her scorn. Blandly, not to give her the satisfaction of real argument, I told her he's too unsophisticated to be pretentious (her claim). His costume is worn for the humble thrill of doing in Rome as Rome does (not that he's heard of the expression)—he actually believes he's dressed *appropriately.* What he hasn't taken in is the idea, dear to the Grobys, that the White Man is supposed to uphold a different set of standards. He's virtually a child, I told her. I didn't mention his drinking habits or his bemused mention of "fucka-girls," and I didn't yet know, last Sunday, about his dealings with them; even if I had, my description of him would have been essentially the same. Obviously at nineteen he was going to be looking for sex somewhere—and it's his gross naiveté that's got him into this scrape. As for Mrs. Groby, that he's Australian is enough to condemn him. A native of Surrey, with a house at Pinner, but having spent most of her adult life following her economist husband to those bits of former Empire that continue to enlist the advice of British "experts," she has led a life of anachronistic Mem-sahibism; her once fair skin's been baked by Africa, India, Hong Kong, to the brown of a cottage loaf's dome. Blue eyes that must have been pretty. Hair the rather strange strawberry blond that gray goes when it's tinted to match the remaining gold of younger days. Figure still good. Accent too good to be true. A paranoid miasma encircles her, and I've learned from others that she's avoided like the plague by all who unavoidably meet her at local teas and cocktails. André, after her first complaining visits to his restaurant, when she kept returning dishes to the kitchen as too hot, too cold, stale, overseasoned, reheated, and so forth, courteously told her not to return if she did not like the food and service. It shut her up and she has been polite on subsequent occasions. As for Duncan, either he's chicken or—more likely, I think—a martyr who knows only too well his wife is sick. He doesn't apologize for her, but he himself does not make offensive remarks. Anyway, he's sending her home to Pinner soon, for a month. They have a son in England.

En route, she informs me, she will have to spend seven hours in Pago-Pago, which according to her is such a revolting place, nothing to do, nothing to see, full of crime and violence, that she will spend the entire day in the airport. I have heard otherwise of Samoa and wish I could stay several days when I go; but I didn't bother to tell her that. Duncan, giving her countenance with an enigmatic, noncommittal remark, languidly let drop that "one might possibly get a decent meal at Soldi's," or some such name.

Since I've seen no newspapers and heard only the sketchiest fragments of radio news for several weeks, I asked Duncan if he'd heard a rumor about a serious spill of plutonium from a nuclear waste-truck convoy in the States, but he pooh-poohed that—only low-level stuff got spilled, nothing important, no one hurt. As an economic adviser he's all for nuclear power. Actually, if he were American I'd guess he was CIA. In any case I got the feeling he's up to no good.

In Perth, a month ago, reading about a Chinese incursion into Vietnam, and about U.S. and Soviet naval vessels loitering off the Vietnam coast, I wondered if IT was about to happen, and—egotistically, but with a sort of languor—whether my death, in the midst of the Great Death nuclear war would mean, was to take place under strange constellations about as far from home as it was possible to be. (In isolation and without the usual sources of daily news, one's relation to world events does seem to erode into this sort of self-centered but unintense speculation.) That passed. Not yet.

Then on my way here, in Suva, Fiji, at the Grand

Pacific Hotel I passed an evening with a very sad, very anxious, homesick Vietnamese. We sat in the lobby in Huey Newton peacock chairs, mosquitoes feasting on my ankles while I listened to his halting French as he told me about his wife (a pharmacologist), their two student sons in Hanoi, the food shortages, the new mobilization, children evacuated once more, his longing for the public health conference he was attending in Fiji to be over so he could get back home. Ceiling fans revolved high over our heads and I flashed back to my Hanoi bedroom and the small dreamy world of its mosquito net, sheltering each night's brief sleep there. It doesn't seem six years or so have gone by since then! I saw tears in his eyes—pressed his cold hands—gave him written greetings to take to my dear friends there.

Just thinking in rapid succession about him, and Elizabeth Groby, and Ray the Australian kid gives me a sort of shudder, a sharp sensation—of dismay is it? Or just a kind of amazement at how fragmented is the human species, and how odd it is to hold in mind, in some kind of unity of perception, individuals so mutually unaware.

After André admitted to pulling my leg about dolphins, he left on some business or other, and Jean-Marie went to the kitchen for my breakfast. The other Frenchmen, my remittance-man friends, Jacques and Pierre and Henri, stayed in town this weekend—ostensibly, and maybe in fact, to take three-hour turns at bailing out their absurd fishing boat, which was launched on Friday after seven months abuilding but ships water like a sieve. Some beguiled relatives in France financed this enterprise, of course, having been persuaded that it might eventually relieve them of the burden of support. Anything to prevent Jacques (or Pierre, or Henri) turning up back in France, God forbid!

The only other guests, in their absence, are from New Zealand, parents and two children who came yesterday for a day at the beach and a birthday dinner for the young mother. He works for Burnes-Phelps, the Australian corporation which sells everything from tractors to toothbrushes, throughout these islands.

I sit reading with my coffee, beginning *Lord Jim*, which some impulse prompted me to snatch from the shelf as I was packing in Somerville, Massachusetts many weeks ago. I never felt inclined to read it before, and brought it less for its approximately appropriate milieu (which I assumed) than because I took it to be about someone dealing with guilt, with knowing he had not done the right thing at some essential moment and that his reasons were not even the damnable "right ones"—the ones one used as justification. . . . Thus far, *Lord Jim* seems rather to be about the *failure* to feel an adequate weight of guilt: it is Marlow who feels it on Jim's behalf. But maybe later, as dénouement perhaps. I had wanted it because I know I ought to have been with my mother at a certain moment during what turned out to be her weeks of dying; and I was not, for no truly defensible reason. I don't *cultivate* guilt—I knew that's a greasy self-indulgence. But I'm searching for inspirations that may serve, a drop here, a drop there, to redress the balance. I want to redeem the loss, not stew in the bitter juice of its memory. If I can.

Lord Jim may not be quite to the point but ah, the prose, the insights! What delight to have such a master-piece with me. And how well it speaks for Paul Scott's *Raj Quartet,* which I finished last night, that even moving immediately from it to the majestic rhetoric of Conrad doesn't make Scott's achievement seem trivial or toneless; not at all. The *Quartet* does not crack or crumble, its edifice stands firm—in a different style of architecture.

I brought the Scott to the island only because I'd begun the first volume before I left home; enthralled, I had to hunt up the rest in Sydney. As it happened, the choice has provided some sidelights here in Tonga. It's not that I see the Raj where it never was; there were obviously many differences in British influence and power in the islands. Aside from anything else, they were never "the jewel in the crown" of empire. Their importance was minimal. But inevitably (though Tonga was called a Protectorate not a Colony) there are traces of Empire's fingers where they lingered, flaccid, among the last stale crumbs of the once enormous pie. And how else describe Mrs. Groby than as a last bastion of that world, even though she is only one of those who flowed into the vacuums left, here and elsewhere, by the withdrawal of persons whose snobbery she imitates but who, in their day, would not have dined with her save under extreme duress?

While I sip my coffee Philemoné comes lilting out of the kitchen and—positively with tears in his eyes— places an ornate necklace of shells about my neck, shakes my hand vigorously, and finally kisses me on both cheeks. Dear, friendly Philemoné! He has been helpful and nice to me throughout my stay; yet he remains a mystery I can't fathom. He looks to be forty-five or fifty and lives in the village a mile away. I'm not sure which of the small boys who appear and disappear among these *fales* clustered around the restaurant are his children, but I know he has a large family. He's the man-of-all-work and appears to be cheerful all the time. The gap between his front teeth is as big, or bigger, than mine, his hair is graying, he's not exactly fat but decidedly plump, and he laughs, indeed giggles, at nothing at all—maybe at life itself. On nights when there are quite a few dinner guests and an outdoor "floorshow" is arranged, he dances. I witnessed this with embarrassment. Done up in sarong and garlands, skipping about more actively than the girls (whose dance consists mainly of arm-movements), wiggling his hips and giving Panto Fairy-queen come-hither beckonings, he is unbelievably camp. It is obvious that traditional island modes are being debased and violated, tricked out in plastic and tinsel for tourists; yet to Philemoné his floorshow is an important event, it seems, and he sees nothing funny about it, though he will laugh uproariously if you happen to say, "It's cooler today" or "Could I have a piece of soap, please?" (It's not easy to tell if this is only because his English is imperfect—I don't mean merely scant, but somehow reversed—or whether things truly strike him as comical for reasons obscure to me or to any foreigner here. There can surely be unknown dimensions of wit, as of other things. Our minds are narrow, narrow and proud. What poetry may not the dolphins, for all we think we know, transmit to one another—and perhaps not by squeaks, which we have begun to read, but by their nudges, the sleek touch of side on side? At all events, Philemoné's farewell enthusiasm, and the necklace, are to express gratitude on behalf of the staff for the little envelope of money I left discreetly on the bar last night for André or Jean-Marie to distribute (fearing there might be no good opportunity this morning). A little later Jean-Marie himself comes to make me a little speech of similar content, but in the formal manner of a graduate of the official French culinary institute. Even sullen Nissi gave me a look slightly less forbidding than usual. Maybe much of her glumness was embarrassment or fright, since I'd spoken sharply to her—I guess one could say I yelled at her!—when she kicked a dog one day. She hadn't really kicked it very hard, but she was giggling at the time, in response to a cat's having almost pulled the cloth off my table and spilled my coffee; and the dog was a bitch nursing puppies. She seemed totally amazed and dismayed at my reaction.

Now I'm beginning to feel disquieted because the Volkswagen bus, which usually goes into town by 9 a.m., is unusually late and I'd told Papiloa I'd be at her house soon after 9. I know I shouldn't worry, time is not important on the island and it is my imminent departure for the U.S. that is making me slip back into that kind of anxiety. Wonderful Papiloa will get me to the plane even if I am a bit late—and the plane probably will leave late anyway.

I met Papiloa in the Auckland airport on my way

here. She'd been at a women's conference in Fiji and then to see a daughter in school in New Zealand. This strong, energetic handsome woman stands out among the sleepy islanders.

I remember the descriptions in *Mariner's Tonga Islands* (1816)—acquired in my childhood with no serious thought that I'd ever be here myself!—and however naive that account may be it certainly doesn't convey the idea of a lethargic population. The long swift canoes, the Tongan's prowess as fishermen and navigators, the many decorative and useful crafts and skills, the variety of good-humoured games: these are what I recall, even though Mr. Mariner's memoirs were filtered through the sententious rhetoric of his ghost-writer, Dr. Martin. But that was before the major mid-Victorian evangelical invasions. The Tongans of Mariner's day may have practiced cannibalism on occasion, but they certainly appear to have been wide awake. I'm sure the listlessness which strikes a visitor today is a symptom of endemic depression.

Life here is not very hard—everyone seems only too well-fed (their diet is overladen with fats and starches) and it is said that a bare stick planted in the soil here (which looks like mere sand) will soon leaf out. The beautiful traditional *fales* have given place, with rare exceptions, to tin-roofed shacks built of cinderblocks; no one is homeless, though. And everyone gets an elementary, and I think some high school, education. Some of the traces left by the British connection are not without charm—for example, the architecture of the modestly-sized Royal Palace, which resembles a miniature

Osborne, Queen Victoria's residence on the Isle of Wight. But the Victorian age, with its Methodist and other Protestant missionaries, eroded the traditional culture and substituted for it the values of the mid-nineteenth century at its English worst, deadly as a wet Sunday in Peckham in 1880. (*Everything* closes down at noon on Saturdays until Monday morning.) There are rules here such as: no swimming on Sundays; men must not go shirtless (no matter how hot and sticky the weather); and others along the same lines. More recently, overfishing has, I'm told, reduced the once-teeming supply and the men no longer go to sea; the canoes are now to be seen only in museums of anthropology. They raise a lot of pigs here, not a laborious task, eat a lot of fat pork, put on weight early and die of heart disease.

But Papiloa has somehow escaped all that. She's an active organizer, trying to wake up her compatriots, especially the women. She talks of teaching them to improve the diet, or cooperatives to relearn, produce, and market the old crafts, of stimulating a demand for opportunities of higher education.

It was she who took me to visit the new "University," an amazing experience. A Tongan man, outstanding as herself, who had managed to leave the island to get a higher education (at least partly in England), has singlehandedly opened what he calls, and intends shall be, a university, consisting so far of a group of converted chicken-houses raised on stilts, on a piece of swamp land no one wanted. When we arrived there, he was lecturing a class of students between the ages of sixteen and perhaps twenty-two. Squeezed into little primary-school desks, these well-grown young men and women, serious and handsome, looked like giant children, both because of the disparity of size and because the challenge and fascination of learning have shaken that pervasive boredom out of them and restored the eager openness of childhood. There were no textbooks, only flimsy mimeo sheets; the subject was—Antigone. This term, the Greeks; next term, Shakespeare.

Next I was introduced to his principal colleague, a tiny silver-haired lady from Aberdeen with a strong, precise enunciation full of rolled R's. How had she landed in this unlikely place, where she (like him) taught a variety of subjects (I believe she told me they were doing the Wars of the Roses in English History)? She had come out to visit her son, it appeared, when he was in the Peace Corps here, and encountering this heroic undertaking at its inception had been inspired to stay on.

The founder's next class was in the Tongan language and history. He also plans to revive the crafts and ceremonies, while at the same time giving his students a general education "comparable to what they could get at Oxford or Cambridge."

Mosquitoes floated in and out of the glassless, sceeenless windows; left-over fowls clucked and crowed among the pilings supporting the narrow classrooms. I shall send them all my extra books when I get home, to help their so-far almost non-existent library.[*] . . . If

---

[*] I did ship a number of mailsacks-full of books to Tonga a few months later but never heard a word more about the University or whether they arrived. I did read, much later, that Papiloa had been elected a Member of Parliament.

what is being attempted here, and what Papiloa is doing among the women, succeed, it could change the life of the island dramatically. I suppose that might mean that things which give pleasure to a visitor like me might change too—things like the fact that the young lady who sits in the Tourist Information booth (a beautiful *fale*) in the center of Nukualofa is in fact the Crown Princess; or the insouciantly erratic schedules of air and boat transportation to and from the island; or the unintentional humor of certain statements in the Visitor Information guide: e.g., "Hotels and tour operators will make arrangements for the hire of horses. Generally there are no saddles available and the horses have not been schooled," or "The Nukualofa Yacht and Motor Boat Club welcomes visiting yachtsmen. The club is not active in sailing or yachting activities but the bar does provide a pleasant meeting place for visitors and locals." And, perhaps my favorite: "*Language.* In general most Tongans speak and understand English so few problems should be experienced and remember a Tongan yes can mean no and vice versa."

One delights in all this, but it is unquestionably patronizing to do so. I'm reminded of the detachment of irony in *Viva Mexico,* that account from a debonair Yankee, Charles Flandreau, of a sojourn there around the turn of the century, which I enjoyed so much when I first read it, but which, after I'd lived in Mexico and seen the poverty and other tribulations of its people, I could no longer read so lightheartedly.

Suddenly, a flurry of activity. André has to get the kitchen marketing done and inspect the famous boat to see what could be done about it, and it has been noticed that the Australians are not up and about and haven't breakfasted. Peter's coral wounds must be examined and Ray must be corralled into seeing the doctor! Someone goes off to rouse them. André is already backing the bus out of its overnight spot; Jean-Marie is discussing the day's vegetables with him. Alissi is combing little Marthe's hair. The 'boys' will have to hurry.

Meanwhile I take my last look at the dark reef, the white and sounding rim of the immense, treacherous ocean beyond it. In the paler shallows within that boundary, swimming two and three times a day, I'd felt the river-like strength of the current pull me sideways past the shore's dazzling green of sand-ivy and the dense darker growth of bread-fruit and avocado trees, above which waved the high-polished fans of aloof coco palms. Walking on my hands like some kind of crab I had peered into miniature caves of dull, dun-colored coral where small fishes of a violet more absolute than the hue of any flower I could remember, and others of sooty velour black, of neon blues and sulfurous lichen yellows, pursued the objects of their appetite with seeming playfulness.

All at once my reverie is broken as Ray, distraught, and Peter soberly attendant, shamble rapidly onto the ramshackle terrace announcing that the five hundred dollars in travelers' checks which Ray still had in hand had gone—vanished. Stolen? But they were not easy to cash. "Do you have the sheet of serial numbers you're supposed to keep separate?" I ask. He doesn't even know what I mean. He has the numbers but only as he himself had written them out; no one seems to have explained, when he bought them, about the safeguard of the official record. "O.K." someone says, "but first, are you sure you've really lost the checks?" "We've looked through everything three times," the boys say— or at least, Ray says; Peter seems to agree it won't hurt to look again. But we're to start off anyway, André insists. We'll ask in town if he dropped the checkbook, report the loss to the police.

My luggage has been loaded while this was going on, and we do start off—the bus full of voices and anxiety and shopping baskets and suitcases. There's a flurry of sand and chickens as we move towards the road—I look back to my hut and at this place I'll never see again. I'll never know if the checks are found, if Ray is cured or deported (maybe all he has is the clap, but syphilis is prevalent around these parts, I've heard), and if the remittance men's boat ever becomes seaworthy. And what will they do it if does? Jacques has given me a Parisian address, and vowed to repay the money I "lent" him, which I knew he and his boy-friend were desperate for: I just felt, oh, what the hell, it's not much, why not cheer him up a bit, I doubt if he'll ever see Paris again.

We pass one of the burying grounds, mounds of sand decorated with tinsel and plastic and old coke-bottles set in circles. It seems amazing that dogs and pigs don't unbury the dead, the loose dry sand looks so easy to shuffle away. In my brief stay here it's as if I'd scuffled a sandy surface—but not come near what lies beneath it. I imagine returning—but know I never shall.

Two hours in town, at most, with Papiloa and at the air field, and then I'll be airborne, looking back at a vanishing green isle in the dark, ironic Pacific. Sounds, sights, sensations, water and light, palmtrees, the night's glowing "serpent" and these people and their lives—all that has been a part of me, and me of it, for a little island of time remote from the personages of my life as this island is from the actual continents—will remain for me an unfinished story. Once I have flown away I will become to them as unreal, as insubstantial and irrelevant a memory as they, and all my days and nights here, will gradually become to me; more so, indeed, for I will have written down at least these scenes and a few poems, and so shall carry with me those reminders, to take my inner eye back to Tonga.

MILDRED

Her profile seemed to have intended to come to a sharp point, but blunted itself before it got there. Her general shape resembled that of a medium-sized, active, young pig, while her coat reminded me of a certain type of doormat in color and texture, although it was curly. With a sort of cunning innocence, or innocent cunning, she took the opportunity, in the moment of chaos she created by giving us her vociferous welcome, to slip into the drawing room—forbidden territory—the instant someone unguardedly opened its door. "Edward!" I yelled, "Come and catch her! Get her out of there!" But Mildred had already located the ball she had hidden behind an armchair and was rushing about, skidding and braking on the slippery floor in perilous glee, the ball now in her mouth, now rolling underfoot. Something fragile was sure to topple and smash in a moment. But Mildred's expressive eyes were full of guileless confidence as she dribbled the ball up to my toes—"Come on," she seemed to say, "Isn't this *fun!*"

Who are you, Mildred, running through the house that was my home from infancy until I married—and which, long gone, is still my essential home in dreams, the archetypal locus? Are you just a composite memory

of dogs I have met? (And why is Edward—a friend of
nowadays—in my mother's kitchen?) Are you a part of
me, Mildred, an animal part, comic, cheerful, trusting,
and obstreperous? Why do I need to be nudged?
Whatever you are, I enjoyed my encounter with you,
and woke from the dream you starred in full of the
words which would make me remember you.

WHAT ONE REMEMBERS

One day when I was eleven or twelve I was hanging around the Covent Garden stage door hoping one of the dancers would emerge into the sweetly rotten air of Floral Street. I was idly watching some of the market-men bustle by, bearing their bizarre untoppling towers of vegetable and fruit baskets, when two portly men stepped out from the stage door. I knew them by sight: one, trimly bearded, was Sir Thomas Beecham, the conductor; the other—larger and rounder, wearing a beret—was the artist Christian Bérard. They were talking animatedly in French about some passage of choreography, and as they moved towards the street corner Sir Thomas illustrated his point by a neatly-performed pirouette, without interrupting the pace of their walk. The moment stands clear amid the blur of those ballet-obsessed days.

But some experiences come too early to be appreciated. At eight years old or less I was taken by my parents to have tea with Paul Robeson and his wife in their London hotel suite: I recall only the elegant room, a brocaded settee placed diagonally at its center, and the impressive tea trolley wheeled in by a waiter. Also that I was wearing my new off-white three-quarter-length coat, tailored by my mother, and my cherished pink hat. Mr. Robeson was big, his wife slender, the atmosphere pleasant. I retained nothing of what was said.

Likewise, Professor Feodotov, who came sometimes from Paris to talk with my father, was to me a rather sweet little man in a grey suit, who wore a pointed beard like my father and whose strong Russian accent I liked to imitate. My sister, though so adult and clever, was not above joining me in a loud game, based on this imitation, to while away long bus rides to and from town. This absurdly absent-minded and otherworldly invention of ours, the fictive Feodotov, would ask all sorts of naive questions about buildings, statues, vehicles, or people that we passed, and his "guide" would answer and be promptly misunderstood; all this was shouted loudly and we would eventually both be shrieking with laughter—so much so that other passengers either started to laugh too or were scandalized; once we almost got put off the bus. That the real Dr. Feodotov was a famous Orthodox theologian didn't come through to me till I was grown up.

Then, connected somehow to what one remembers, there are those proofs of the theory that everyone on earth is only about three people away from everyone else—there being links of some kind between them all; those people one does not actually meet but whom a family member or close associate knows, so that their names and the fact of their existence enter one's early life somehow, and are taken for granted there like familiar furniture. Franz Werfel is an instance: very early in my childhood my father was working on a translation of Werfel's play *Paulus unter den Juden—Paul Among the Jews*. They corresponded, his name was spoken frequently during mealtime conversation, he sent my parents a large signed photograph of himself (now in Stanford's Green Library). The play was published, and the Stage Society put it on, with a cast that included Laurence Olivier, Robert Speaight, Abraham Sofaer, Richard ("Dickie") Goolden, and other well-known actors. This was when I was much too young to be taken to see it, but I do just remember the event since it was one of the very rare occasions when my parents and sister all went out for the evening and I was put to bed by the maid.

Much later, when I was about nine, my sister organized an amateur dramatic company and put on two performances of "Paul" at Ilford Town Hall. Rehearsals took place in our house and garden, and for weeks we referred to the young men who acted in it by names of the characters they played. Over fifty years later one of them, "Gamaliel," wrote to me and I've since visited him in East Sussex. When I was twenty and had made friends with Charles Wrey Gardiner at Grey Walls Press I interested him in reprinting the play. It came out with a dust-jacket designed by Lucian Freud, someone else I never met but with whom I acquired two points of contact: this dust-jacket, with its stylized depiction of St. Paul (not at all to my parents' taste); and the raincoat the artist had left at the house of a boyfriend of mine one time and never retrieved, and which after many months I annexed. I used to wear it cinched tightly with a wide Moroccan belt of stamped red and white leather which I'd been assured was a camel-belt—that is, designed to help one deal with the vigorous shaking experienced when riding a camel. . . . I wore it in Holland in the bitter winter of 1946–47; and arrived in Paris that April still clothed in what I thought of then as Freud's grandson's coat, for Lucian the artist was not yet so famous.

But though Werfel was a household name throughout my early years—whose novel about the Armenian massacre of 1915, *The Forty Days of Musa Dagh,* my mother read aloud to us in the evenings when it came out in 1934 or 1935 (editing out a few bits my father felt were too strong for me to hear)—it was not until long afterward that I learned of his connection with so many other artists in whom by then I had become interested, or that his wife had also been the wife of Gustav Mahler and Walter Gropius.

There was also—among such tenuous but often lifelong connections or almost-connections—Eliot—T. S. Eliot, of whom I early heard mention as he was on some committee or other on which my father also served, as well as because my sister was reading *Poems 1909-1925.* I knew, too, that he edited *Criterion,* a magazine my sister sometimes must have bought, for at twelve years old, familiar with certain memorable lines from "The Love Song of J. Alfred Prufrock" and "Preludes," etc., even if so much of their significance necessarily escaped me, I took it into my head to send him some of my poems, secretly or at least *privately* written, and hitherto shown to no one. (His helpful and encouraging reply, received a month or two later when I'd almost forgotten this sudden, isolated act, disappeared eventually, after I'd married and gone to America.) I never approached him again; but my mother gave me *Four Quartets* for my twenty-first birthday, and the following year, when I used to visit John Hayward in the Carlyle Mansions flat he shared with Eliot, I would hear him let himself in and go along the corridor to his own quarters. As I let myself out (Mr. Hayward was in a wheelchair and could not see me to the door), I would see Mr. Eliot's hat and rolled umbrella on the hall stand. For me, he came to exemplify the shadow figures who (themselves unaware) hover at the edges of one's life, not quite entering it, yet encountered more than once, at intervals.

Other events, more remote, seem nevertheless filaments connecting one to figures long-dead: that my father had seen Kropotkin in the British Museum Reading Room when he first came to London, some years before he and my mother first met in Constantinople, gives me such a sense of linkage, however flimsy: as does knowing that Israel Zangwill told my Welsh mother, to her delight, that she had "a Jewish soul."

Certain childhood theatrical experiences are among those that come too soon to be evaluated and savored, yet remain as a kind of historical trophy: Barbette the trapeze artist, all in pink, so feminine, a sort of gymnastic princess—and then at the end of the performance, off comes the golden wig, revealing the bald head of a man! Argentina the great Flamenco dancer: only my mother's and sister's enthusiasm stayed in my mind: her performance bored me. A musical, *Casanova,* in which there was a wonderful revolving stage—that *did* thrill me! Nellie Wallace in "panto" as Aladdin's mother, the Widow Twankey—a very dim memory; indeed, one that would have been entirely forgotten if it were not for my sister's later long-lasting "crush'" on Miss Wallace, whom she followed around and got to know. I remember better my very first theater experiences: *Alice in Wonderland,* after which I sobbed and stormed in the frustration of my desire to go home with "Alice" whom I thought really was a long-haired little girl not so much bigger than me: and the Salzburg Marionettes, seen from the theater's upper balcony and whom I fully believed were actual tiny people, fairies of some kind.

There were backstage visits to Sybil Thorndike (who corresponded with my mother) and Emlyn Williams, who had attended the same high school in Wales where my mother had previously been first a student then a "pupil-teacher." (When we went to Wales for the holidays we called on the teacher who had encouraged him and was the original of the teacher in *The Corn is Green.)* Sometimes stage sets and costumes made more impression on me than the plays themselves (or the players, if I met them): a wonderful split-level set for some play in which Edith Evans and Sybil Thorndike could be seen simultaneously in different rooms, or the rich medieval costumes by Motley for an historical drama. My really rich dramatic experiences came in my teens when I saw, mainly with my friend Betty, but sometimes with my parents, such memorable performances of Chekhov, Shaw, Ibsen, Shakespeare . . . .

Edith Evans, Peggy Ashcroft, Gielgud and Olivier, Marius Goring, Lucy Mannheim, Frederick Valk were among the staple performers in these productions.

Perhaps in the 1990's when lethal violence is so common it is not unusual to know one is only at one remove from a murderer who was, as English law puts it, "hanged by the neck until he is dead," but certainly no one else I knew in my youth had that unhappy connection. And indeed, I was shielded from the knowledge at the time. I remembered little Pauline because she was a delightful friend, and later because of a photo showing us both posed by the Albert Memorial. She and I were among the juvenile participants in a big all-London church pageant held at the Albert Hall. Dressed in chiffon tunics we cavorted, with others (among them teen-age girls like my sister), in a type of skipping and more or less graceful arm-movements known as Greek Dancing. ("About as Greek as my left foot," commented my mother, who, however, willingly ran up our costumes on her little Singer.) The scene, I suppose, represented Ancient Greek Religion. Other religions, past and present, were presented in other episodes, and, casting aside his dignity as Dr. Levertoff, well-known cleric and theologian, my father, bless his heart, played the part of a Whirling Dervish in the scene about Sufism. (Perhaps it felt in tune with the Hasidic dancing he had known as a boy, and into which he would break, to our delight, on joyful special occasions.)

Pauline was a very pretty and gentle little girl, slightly younger and smaller than I (and much less rough and loud than I often was). We became great

friends in the brief period of the rehearsals and perfor-
mance, enjoying tentative explorations of the coulisses
of the great coliseum-like hall, and especially the long
bus rides back to Ilford. She lived, I think, in Seven
Kings, a few stops further on than the Ilford Broadway
one where we got off, and I don't think we ever had the
chance to visit at each other's houses. She too had an
older sister; and also possessed a much older brother
who must either have been in the pageant like us and
our sisters or, more likely, came to escort them home
after rehearsals and the performance itself, for I know I
saw him—a handsome face with well-marked eyebrows.
Perhaps he had acted in my sister's production of *Paul
Among the Jews.*

When the pageant and its excitement were over, our
elders said we would surely visit one another to play
again. But I was distracted by the summer holidays, for
which we went away to the country, and it was quite a
while after our return before I thought to ask about my
playmate—only to be told that alas, her family had
moved away, so it was unlikely we'd meet again. Or
perhaps my mother's answer was more vague than that,
for I don't remember acute disappointment. At six years
old one's sense of the passage of time is not fixed and
the present moment occupies most of one's attention.

In fact I never did see Pauline again, but it was only
when I was an adult that I heard the sad story of why
her family had moved. The grown-up brother had con-
spired with another young man to rob an elderly couple
living somewhere down in the Essex marshes; and
caught in the act, the brother had panicked and killed

them both. His friend ran, but was caught and confessed; and the brother was immediately found and charged. He pled guilty and was sentenced. It had been headlined in all the papers, and Pauline's stricken family moved to another part of the country and changed their name. I wonder if Pauline was protected, as a child, from the knowledge of his hanging, and only learned of it years later, like me? But she must, even at six years old, have picked up so much of the misery around her— and perhaps overheard the truth even if the adults around her supposed her to be absorbed in her dolls.

To me she has retained a vivid reality far beyond that of any famous persons I saw as a child. Does she, perhaps, also have a copy of that snapshot she and I posed for, the Albert Memorial rising above it like some barnacle-encrusted object salvaged from the deep sea? We are dressed alike and both have long, dark, curly tresses; but I look luckier than Pauline: bigger and stronger. She has a fragile look. Did she survive the war? Did her charm and sweet nature survive the tragedy that drove her family to some place unknown? Was it hard for her to learn a new surname? Did she forget her oldest brother whom no one spoke of any more? If she's alive—close to seventy now—does she recall our long bus rides, eastward on the #25 through the thrilling London evenings, and wonder as I do what we talked about so tirelessly, so happy in our companionship?

A LOST POEM

I had seen cathedrals, and I had lived a while in Florence, where the trams ground clanging past the grandeur of the Duomo in January's icy mists. I had read somewhere of a king's ransom in jewels decorating the carved saints in Peru or Brazil, where Indios shuffled on their knees towards them, like those I had seen in Mexico, in the shadows and golden candlelight of enormous colonial churches. And in a dream these things danced together and reassembled: I saw a vast cathedral advance its majestic prow into a small piazza or zocalo that was the very heart of its city. Round it, all day, and far into the night, the noisy tramcars labored, drudging busily as tugboats, tiny and puerile below that solemn height, ringing their urgent bells. Within them the crowds—and the cars were always crowded—all gazed up at the façade, and leaned out of the open sides towards it, stretching out their hands. The tramline passed so close that they could actually touch it—touch that famous and extraordinary wall of riches. For this was the fabled Cathedral of Pearls: the entire façade was a cliff encrusted with pearls—its smallest interstices filled with seed pearls, its planes and cornices and whole height studded with pearls of every size; pearls the size of bantam eggs gracing the crowns and breastplates of the virgin martyrs, the archangels, black pearls and pink among the white, the whole dress of the madonna a soft luminescence of pearls. And all day—through years, through centuries—the brown hands of the poor reached out to touch them: not to take them but only to touch them, caressively, with awe and affection. Never was one pearl missing.

That was the dream, and I remember writing it as a poem—"Cathedral of Pearls." Though the poem was published, I believe in some fugitive magazine, it is more than thirty years ago and I have lost all trace of it. If it ever turns up, like another poem I thought lost, a poem about Swiss peasants, men, women and children, returning to their valley after a harvest day in the mountain pastures—will it tell me anything more, anything I have forgotten? What remains with me is not the idea— though that cannot fail to occur—that the poor would be less poor if the cathedral were stripped bare and the pearls sold, but the sense of the murky darkness of the city even in daylight, the darkness of the stone in which the pearls were embedded, the glimmering beauty of the pearls—magical barnacles upon a great vessel risen from the sea—and the deep pleasure that beauty was to those who passed and repassed.